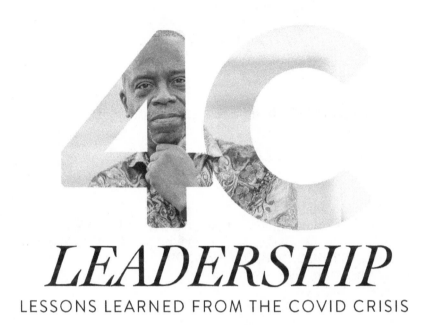

LEADERSHIP

LESSONS LEARNED FROM THE COVID CRISIS

COURTNEY MCBATH

4C Leadership: Lessons Learned from the COVID Crisis
by Courtney McBath

copyright ©2020 Courtney McBath
ISBN: 978-1-950718-60-3

Printed in the United States of America

4C Leadership is available in Amazon Kindle, Barnes & Noble Nook and Apple iBooks.

Scripture marked NASB taken from the NEW AMERICAN STANDARD BIBLE®, Copyright © 1960,1962,1963,1968,1971,1972,1973,1975,1977,1995 by The Lockman Foundation. Used by permission.

CONTENTS

INTRODUCTION

Crises tend to be the training ground for leadership. Wars produce great presidents and prime ministers. Oppression becomes the breeding ground for liberators and activists. Troubled times seem to be the harvest season for greater leaders and leadership.

This is not the least coincidental—adversity births greatness. People rise to their best when trouble comes; and as they arise, they begin to believe that anything is possible. The desperation produced by storms, disease, terrorism, war, and other tragedies produces leaders and leadership strategies. In times of peace—in the absence of traumatic circumstances—leadership principles are essential. But in times of adversity, these principles are beyond important: They carry life-and-death potential.

As we globally face COVID-19, leaders and leadership are rising. We are understanding principles that we never realized—or at least ones we had not been forced to implement. At 60 years of age, I can say that I have never walked through anything like this. The terrorist attacks of 9/11 were devastating, but they did not create shortages in food and medical supplies, sweeping international fear and death, and global lockdown.

As you read this book, take note of the practical lessons that all of us are learning. We have experienced great training in "peacetime," but nothing can compare to the lessons learned in "wartime." The beauty of strategies born out of trouble is that they find application at all times. Unfortunately, much of what we learn in peacetime just doesn't apply in seasons of overwhelming adversity. The principles and strategies—the 4 Cs of leadership—that you learn here will not only give you tools to lead by, but they will remind you that, in the darkest times of your life, you learn what you could not learn otherwise.

I continue to pray for you as you navigate this season—that you will daily discern applications that are life-changing for you and for those you influence.

—*Courtney McBath*

THE POWER OF CONTEXT

CHAPTER 1

KNOWING WHOM WE ARE LEADING AND INFLUENCING

I never fully understood the power of context until I had to lead during a time of acute crisis and adversity. Only then did I realize how critical it is to know and understand where you're leading and whom you're influencing in detail. When we're not in crisis, we have the luxury of doing what we think is cool, or what we find fulfilling, but that luxury dissipates quickly in crisis. Resources are limited, and time becomes a rare commodity. While our work can be fulfilling, decisions can no longer be made solely based upon what makes the leader happy.

Context is defined as "the circumstances that form the setting for an event, statement, or idea, and in terms of which it can be fully understood and assessed." Context is the accurate description of all that surrounds the sphere in which you're leading. Context speaks to the demographics of communities—the economic and educational institutions and the conditions in which people live. Contextualization includes understanding how people think, communicate, and make decisions. These facts don't change no matter how much we pray, preach, or push!

Jesus constantly made decisions about what He would do based on the context He was in. There were places in which He refused to perform many miracles because those cities were not open to His ministry. Matthew 13:58 says, "And He did not do many miracles there because of their unbelief." Jesus healed some people, but very few miracles were performed in his hometown, not because He was limited, but due to the context of their unbelief. If Jesus limited His actions based on context, how much more do we need to, at the very least, adjust our methods based on our own surroundings?

One of the fundamental differences between leading in crisis and leading where no immediate crisis exists is the significance of knowing whom you're leading. It can be argued that context is more important, in all circumstances, than we realize. However, the critical nature of contextualizing leadership is easier to ignore when there is no crisis. In other words, you may be able to get away with not knowing your target audience when there is no danger, but in adversity, you must know whom you're leading and what they need in order to succeed.

There are times in which we take a "shotgun" approach in our leadership, and simply hope that someone is being touched or helped by our efforts. Our motives are pure and our hearts are clean, but we lack any specific sense of strategy. We hope and pray that we are doing good, and this is honorable, but it may prove ineffective. During times of peace and tranquility, one can afford to try this or try that and hope for good results. However, even in peaceful settings, this creates a leadership motivated by feeling good, not by the results. This can happen in churches, parachurch ministries, nonprofit organizations, and even for-profit businesses. Leaders stop being guided by results, and begin to be directed by an individual's preference or a team's sense of fulfillment. Oftentimes, as long as there is money and materials to continue, a leader continues to lead when no one is following. But we know the old saying:

If you think you're leading but no one is following, you're just taking a walk!

Unless there is a major paradigm shift, you can "lead" in this manner indefinitely. Unfortunately, most organizations that find themselves in the stages of plateau and decline have lost their sense of context. They have lost sight of their targeted audience—those whom they are actually called to touch—and the most effective ways to reach that audience.

There are three levels of knowledge you must assess in crisis in order to succeed. Even when you're leading outside of a crisis, it will benefit you greatly to consider each of these.

KNOW THE "FELT" NEEDS

The group's "felt" needs are the things they feel they need. You may feel they need a relationship with God, but if they are food-insecure, they won't feel what you feel. If you don't learn how to address the need they feel, you will never get a chance to meet the needs *you* think they have.

When there is no crisis—when resources are bountiful and there is no strong sense of desperation—it's easier to start working on what you feel is needed. You don't necessarily need research, interviews, or data. You can begin to do things that make you feel like you're really helping. However, if you're going to succeed in your leadership position during crisis, you have to know what people actually need. You have to know what they are longing for. You have to know what keeps them up at night. You have to know what makes them worry. Even if, ultimately, your leadership is not equipped to meet all of their felt needs, you will be more successful because you will demonstrate an empathy that can only come from knowing the felt needs of those you desire to lead.

One of the felt needs during this recent crisis was the ability to be tested for the Coronavirus in a non-invasive manner.

Now, as a leader, I may want to provide Bibles to people—and there's nothing wrong with giving Bibles, but if I can push for testing centers for people who need to know their condition, they may be much more open to my Christian witness.

KNOW YOUR OWN CAPACITY

Since so many leaders are ignorant of the felt needs of the people they want to influence, they also fail to understand their capacity to meet those needs. It's a simple premise:

If I don't know what's needed, I won't know if I'm capable of meeting the needs.

Capacity can be measured in a number of different ways, but for our simple analysis, we will say that our capacity is the accurate assessment of our *resources, competencies,* and *vision. Resources* are comprised of the people, leadership, finances, and influence that can be leveraged to produce results. *Competencies* speak to sheer human ability or personnel resources, and what we bring to bear in both voluntary and paid staff. While resource addresses if we have enough, competency addresses if we are good enough. *Vision* is a huge factor in understanding one's capacity. I can have resources and competency, but if I have no vision or passion for what people need, I won't be effective as a leader.

KNOW YOUR VISION AND PASSION

Not everyone has the same calling, capability, or capacity. Not everyone has the same vision or passion. When you've been strategically or divinely placed in a certain space, your heart will have vision and passion to meet the needs of that space. Where there is no vision or passion, people do what seems right to them.

Ultimately, what governs the human activity is what the mind sees (vision) and what the heart feels (passion).

It is possible to see a need, have the capability to meet it, but lack the vision and passion to execute your plan. Never try to take on a need that you have no passion for—no matter how noble the cause. During crisis, one of the many leadership lessons you'll learn is that you have to position leaders within their areas of passion. Adversity drains the heart, mind, and body. If there is no passion, leaders don't last! In order to improve the long-term stamina of those who are helping, it's best to try to match people with their passions. Passion supplies emotional energy that makes a significant impact on the long-term process. Apply this principle to yourself and those you lead! Everyone, including those you serve, will be more content when you properly match people and their passions with needs and expectations.

KNOW YOUR AUDIENCE

Context means understanding who's in your audience. Crisis teaches us that, in order to get people to listen, be led, and lend you a hand, you need to know who is in your audience. Every decision to touch lives, speak life, save lives, or lead lives stems from the knowledge of whom it is you're talking to.

Within the context of your sphere of influence, there are people who will listen to you. Listening to you is where everything begins. If you want to encourage your sphere, it begins with people hearing you. Actually, they are already listening to you. Your responsibility is to speak the language of your audience. While your message remains the same, how you deliver that message will change based on your audience. If you want to teach, coach, provide, or train people, it starts with them hearing you. Whatever you are hoping to accomplish, it begins with a clear message, and clarity of message is the result of using the language spoken by your audience. Language truly shapes culture.

Those who listen to you will be the same people who allow you to lead them. This is the context in which you lead. At no other time does this truth become more obvious than in crisis. Crisis makes us think in practical terms—every step must be a pragmatic one. Leadership in crisis is never for the sake of appearances: People's lives are at stake. When carried into every season of leadership, this pragmatic paradigm is extremely effective. It assists the leader in determining the value of the decisions made based on how they produce results, not how elegant or impressive they are. Identify who actually listens to you, and then you will know whom you can lead.

In crisis and out of it, there is something every leader needs to know. Who will lend a hand? It's awesome that people listen and are willing to be led, but your greatest need is resources. Whether you need volunteers, social media engagement, financial contributions, or volunteer hours, context teaches you who will lend you a hand in fulfilling the vision. Understanding this will help you craft your message for the people in your context, so you can effectively ask for what they are able to give. If my context is college students, I might not want to ask for major financial contributions. I may be more successful asking for volunteer hours or social media engagement. But if I don't know my context, I may send an inappropriate message—a message that either my hearers don't understand or one which they lack the will or ability to respond to. In crisis, these lessons are underscored because you don't have time to waste on messages that get no results.

Do your homework and fully understand the context in which you're leading. Knowing your demographics, social media data, and what makes sense in your situation will save you time and frustration.

CHAPTER 2

UNDERSTANDING THE EXISTING TRUST LEVEL

In every context, there exists a level of trust (or mistrust). More often than not, this trust level has direct ties to those who are presently involved in leadership within your context. You learn quickly in difficult times that little can be accomplished where there is little trust. Stephen Covey writes, "When trust is low, change is slow and costly, when trust is high then change is faster and less expensive."[1] The word "change" can be used interchangeably with the word "progress" or "success." When you properly contextualize the sphere in which you are called to lead, you must account for and assess the trust level. Once you make that assessment, you can build on the trust that exists and improve the areas in which you discover a trust deficit.

IMPROVING TRUST

Trust seems so ethereal that we can assume it's intangible—or, at least, that it's some soft, warm, fuzzy word that can't possibly be quantified. This is not true. Some of the greatest business, military, and government leaders in history have identified the idea of trust as "critical to operations!"

Trust can be measured; therefore, trust can be improved. Covey notes that, "the greatest myth about trust is that you can't do anything about it if it's not there."[2]

Every relationship in life is in some way tied to trust: every business transaction; every investment; every marriage; every vote. I could go on, but you understand. Trust is the bedrock of all human transactions, and distrust is most often the reason why transactions don't happen or relationships don't last. It is impossible to discuss the contextualization of the place in which you lead without discussing why trust is critical to leadership. In crisis, it becomes clear that all leadership is about change: leading people from danger to safety, from discouragement to courage, from sickness to health. Change is the order of the day in crisis, and it's an underlying need outside of crisis, as well. Danger, war, and disease underscore the human need to move from point A to point B with the minimum amount of risk. How does the human soul make these calls? We determine whom we can trust.

Therefore, in order to lead effectively you must know where the trust needle sits on the gauge of the organization you lead. Once you know where the deficit is, you must take control of adjusting trust.

If you examine John C. Maxwell's teaching on levels of leadership, you will discover that the lowest level of leadership is positional leadership: when people follow you because you're the president, the pastor, the owner, or the check-signer. Most people in the world, unfortunately, are leading from this place. "Position is the lowest level of leadership—the entry level. The only influence a positional leader has is that which comes with the job title. People follow because they have to."[3]

Positional leadership doesn't require skills, results, or trust. Anyone can hold a position. While it's a good place to start, you don't want to stay there. In Maxwell's pyramid of leadership, you move from positional to pinnacle. Every step up requires a greater infusion of trust. At the pinnacle level, you're training other leaders—and leaders will not be led by someone they don't trust.

If we are unable to see trust grow, we will never escape the low point of positional leadership, but because we do control the needle of trust, we can leave positional leadership and move to relational leadership. This is leadership that has little to nothing to do with position, but has everything to do with trust.

BECOME MORE TRUSTWORTHY

While you cannot force people to trust beyond their own limitations, you can increase the trust level in your context. This change doesn't begin with your company or your ministry—it begins with you! When the leader focuses on becoming trustworthy, it has a domino effect on your organization and, ultimately, impacts the community in which you serve.

LIVE A CONGRUENT LIFE

Congruency, or harmony, is another way of describing integrity. When who you are externally matches who you are internally, there is congruency. As you live life being true to yourself, it shows, just as the converse also shows. You won't have to announce it or brag about it—people will just know. It will seep out of the pores of your life. Tom Peters said it best: "Ask yourself . . . mercilessly: Do I exude trust? E-x-u-d-e. Big word. Do I smack of 'trust'? Think about it. Carefully."[4]

Congruence, like integrity, does not say that you're perfect, but rather that you live in harmony with your deepest beliefs. Your so-called values are not constantly in conflict with your actions. Check your finances, how you pay your debts, your closest personal relationships and the consistency with which you keep your word. Be relentlessly tough on yourself in this area.

LIVE A SELFLESS LIFE

Make it clear that your agenda is others first and not self first. People trust those who live life intentionally to bless others. Jesus referred to the best leaders as servants first. As your organization sees your "not my personal agenda" kind of life, they will trust you and follow your example.

The late Kobe Bryant commanded my trust. Back in 2009, I took my youngest son, Xavier, to see the man he considered the all-time greatest athlete when the Lakers played the Philadelphia 76ers at the Staples Center. As the game came down to the end, it was extremely close, and to everyone's surprise (including Jack Nicklaus), Andre Iguodala turned at the top of the key and nailed a game-winning jumper for Philly. At this point, the meet-up my referee friend had planned for my son with Kobe after the game was totally in question. I had no expectation that, after losing a buzzer-beater at home, Bryant would do interviews, let alone come to talk to a kid he had never met. But we waited in the hallway, just in case.

After nearly an hour, a tall, handsome 27-year-old man came strolling down the hallway, greeted me and my two sons with a smile, and spent the next 20 minutes laughing and talking with us like we were old friends. That's a selfless life. Kobe's agenda was not his own disappointment in a loss, but the thrill of giving a young fan a once-in-a-lifetime experience.

I have always trusted Kobe Bryant.

LIVE A CAPABLE LIFE

People trust the competent. Those who are good at what they do seem to command respect.

As important as congruency and selflessness are, they can't replace competency. Whenever you raise the bar of your own performance, you increase the level of trust that others place in you. In times of crisis, when failed leadership can result in loss of life, people are adamant about the capabilities of those who lead them. Being boisterous, outspoken, or well-spoken are not a "get out of jail free" card for the inability to lead well. Capable leaders prepare themselves emotionally, mentally, and strategically for the battles ahead. You don't get the sense that this is their first rodeo—they walk in ready to go.

While well-equipped leaders seem to steer the ship naturally and with ease, you can be sure that it took many years of hard work, suffering, and intentional preparation to get to that place—preparation birthed from an honest assessment that exposes areas requiring continual improvement. What's interesting about leadership is how the same leaders who were so busy they could hardly keep up before crisis are the same leaders who are pulled on the most during crisis. Rather than utilize other leaders who now have plenty of time, people reach out to the leaders who have more to offer than they know how to handle. Why? Because the competent are always in demand!

LIVE AN EFFECTIVE LIFE

Nothing builds trust like a life that demonstrates tangible results. Context is impacted by trust. In crisis, only those who trust the leader will listen to, be led by, and lend a hand with his or her vision. If you want to minimize distrust, you must be able to prove (beyond just words) that you will get the job done. That's why every task is so critical. Each responsibility prepares you for the next hurdle, and helps to establish the credibility that only comes through empirical data: cold, hard proof.

Remind yourself never to look at any initiative as a waste of time or too insignificant to do. As parents often tell their children, "Any job worth doing is worth doing well."

In one of my graduate-level courses, we were asked to do something many considered extremely morbid: The professor asked us to write our own obituaries. I took this assignment seriously and wrote painstakingly—detail after detail. I wrote my age when I died, who would sing and preach at my funeral, and what my wife would wear. Still, deep down, I wrestled with the *why* of this request. When it came time to turn in our work, there was an animated class discussion. Finally, the professor asked us, "Do you know why you did this?" We didn't, so he told us: "Now that you have determined the circumstances of your death, go live in a way that will make your obituary come true!" If you want a reputation for being effective, then make every task count and get results.

23

PROMOTE A VISION THAT SCREAMS "PEOPLE MATTER!"

The people in your context may not know much about you personally, but they know your vision. At the very least, they know the parts of your vision that impact them. Your vision tells people what you're truly about, because it determines how you spend all your resources. Your time, talent, and treasure are all meted out according to a well-articulated vision (or, conversely, one that's never spoken).

The amount of trust in the sphere where you have been called to serve is elevated when you have a vision that makes it abundantly clear that people matter. In the recent pandemic, I constantly made this statement to my church: "We will not come out of this known for being a church that brought in enough money to keep the bills paid. We will have a reputation for loving people, feeding people, and meeting their needs."

It wasn't surprising to us that we remained a vibrant, effective site to distribute food to the food-insecure. We had already established a vision that shouted daily, "PEOPLE MATTER!"

PREPARE LEADERS WITH HUMBLE, HOLY AMBITION

The folks in the community may never have met you. Clients and customers may not know you personally, but they know your staff and those who represent you. In order to raise contextual trust, volunteers, paid staff, and leaders must have holy ambition. Is there such a thing? Isn't ambition by its very name "unholy"? Absolutely not!

The *Oxford American Dictionary* defines ambition as "a strong desire to do or to achieve something, typically requiring determination and hard work." What makes ambition holy? Humility! When your teams are hungry to succeed, relentless to operate in excellence, and anxious to achieve greatness for the good of others, that is HOLY! When senior leaders and all those who are connected to them are operating with a vision to serve, you will see new levels of trust!

CHAPTER 3

ASSESSING THE CONTEXTUAL NEED

This chapter holds a question-and-answer format designed to get you analyzing your specific area of influence—business or ministry. If you take copious notes, you can improve everything from your donor base to your relationship with your spouse and/or children. Let's do this!

IS CONTEXT IMPORTANT?

The power of contextualization is an untapped resource for many leaders. It's often thought of as an important strategy for large companies: Know your market, know your customer, know your audience. Context is important in any and every situation. Ministries need to understand their surroundings—and nothing highlights this need quite like a crisis. During crisis, I discovered that, in spite of the

1500 young adults in our church, our median age of active partners was 55. That meant when I talked about the use of technology for small groups, teaching, or giving, a significant part of my audience had to make a paradigm shift in order to follow me.

Consider the power of understanding context in your family. Many of us grew up with computers that sat on a desk or in our laps. Today's children have the same computing power in their phones! How does this change family communication dynamics? You send emails and write on paper; they send text messages. By understanding how differently your kids communicate, you can improve your effectiveness with them by "speaking their language."

Don't underestimate this context discussion, or throw it into your mental "Spam" file. Whether you're a parent raising a family, a pastor shepherding a church, or a leader of a nonprofit organization, contextualization is critical to your leadership effectiveness.

WHOM ARE YOU REACHING (OR TRYING TO REACH)?

Dr. Sam Chand says, "The first thing you have to align in your organization is the people. Unless you get the 'who' right, the 'what' is irrelevant."[5] This not only speaks to your team, but also your audience (or the audience you hope to reach). Take the time to learn details about those to whom you're speaking—who they are will determine what you say and how you say it. Are they young or mature in age? Are they wealthy or struggling financially? Are they technolog-ically astute, or is technology a challenge for them? Do they have formal education or on-the-job certifications?

My list of questions is inexhaustible, and you can't ask or answer every one. My concern is for leaders who ask *no* questions about those they say they are called to touch: lead-ers who are well-acquainted with their message but poorly connected to the recipients. At times, it appears these lead-ers only want to speak, but have no interest in being heard. While this is acceptable for the ego, it does little to reach peo-ple, sell products, or solve problems. Crisis teaches us that what doesn't work is unnecessary.

HOW DOES YOUR CONTEXT COMMUNICATE?

When you think of the people you need to influence do you ever think about how they best communicate? There will be a percentage of them who prefer to get their infor-mation a particular way, but they may not represent the whole. The transfer of information is one of the most crit-ical activities in any organization. However, it's a useless activity if not executed in a way that reaches people. Every scenario is different. You may need to think email versus snail mail. Someone else may need to think email versus text messaging. Still someone else needs to consider text messaging versus face-to-face. Take the time to think about the people you influence (or want to influence) and the best ways to reach them.

One size does not fit all, so a plethora of communication methods is helpful. You can say the same thing but package it in different ways. An email to lots of my donors can say "Thank you." Then, I can send text messages to another group, and handwritten cards to another. The message is the same in every medium, but what good is the message if it never arrives at the hearers' hearts?

Communication is not just a matter of the means or media—we must analyze frequency. Does your constituency like to talk? Would they like to hear from you daily, weekly, monthly, or annually? As in our earlier discussion, everyone is different; you will discover that people in the same family may have two different appetites for communication with you. I suggest that, rather than spending money, time, and energy trying to figure out who uses what and when, set up various frequencies and let your people choose which one they prefer. Emails, live talks on social media, and even meetings give people options: to read or not, to show up or not. Now, you have made it possible for the person who wants more to have more, and for the person who prefers less to choose less.

Communication strategies must also address our context's level and means of comprehension. Some will absorb concepts, facts, and vision at a higher rate than others. Some will more readily comprehend what they can touch and feel, while others easily grasp words and abstract ideas. Everyone is important, no matter how they are wired to comprehend. So it becomes the leader's responsibility to make sure important information is easily understood by all. We call that, "putting the cookies on the lower shelf"—and if you're somewhat vertically challenged like me you have a deep appreciation for cookies you can reach!

HOW DOES YOUR CONTEXT RELATE TO TECHNOLOGY?

In today's world, technology is the way of the world. Technology moves ahead so quickly that the phone you hold in your hand may undergo a complete operating system change three months after you purchase it. Technology is not only helpful and convenient—it can also be daunting. How tech-savvy is the group of people that will determine your success? As we have found in every cursory examination of context so far, no group of people is monolithic. There are huge variations within groups. Not all young people, older people, black people, or white people are the same.

Take extreme care lest you fail to recognize the deep variations that exist in every group of humans. In today's world, you can assume that most are impacted by technology, and have some experience with it—you just may not know exactly how much. Take the time to study your demographic and understand how most will respond if you say, "Just download this app." How will they respond if you write, "All the information you need is in this link"?

Since we can't do much without the use of technology, be prepared to train those who don't have someone to help them. Set up a Genius Bar at the church, the food pantry, or the counseling center. I have found that, by remaining sensitive and providing help, I've been able to improve someone's quality of life while simultaneously helping that person locate my product, training, or simply some encouragement.

WHAT ARE THE FEARS OF YOUR CONTEXT?

You may be amused or taken aback by this question. It may seem a bit personal. You're probably right, but crisis teaches us that fear impedes progress. The leader who is adept in every setting will be keenly aware of what scares people. During crisis, I listen carefully to the words of unsympathetic leaders. They frequently use words like "death" instead of "losses" or "fatalities." Amazingly, they have no idea of the fear they create with their words. Since words shape culture, they unknowingly build a culture of fear. Wise leaders are empathetic; they sense the fears and fear triggers of the people they want to influence, and devote themselves to protecting those hearts from fear.

In crisis, people have a much deeper fear of death. This makes the leader's task infinitely more difficult. He or she must protect people from their fear, while at the same time being honest with them about the circumstances. If a leader attempts to reduce fear through lies, it will ultimately create more fear, because now, the people must fear the crisis *and* the onslaught of false information. The effective leader does not fabricate falsities to protect from fear. He or she learns to speak the truth in love. Since communication is 95% non-verbal, the saying is true: "It's not what you say, it's *how* you say it." When a leader has empathy, even in sharing difficult truth, people feel protected, fear is minimized, and courage is released.

Outside of a pandemic or war, we all have our own sets of individual fears. Many of these fears we share. In fact, families often share fears. Never forget that life can be scary. Your role is to take some of the fright out of life in the context in which you are called to lead.

WHAT DO YOU HAVE IN COMMON WITH YOUR COMMUNITY?

You and your organization will have more in common with your context than not. Whether you feel placed in a community by Divine Providence or by chance, you'll discover that you tend to lead where you find a sense of commonality. People tend to make more sales, create more donors, and lead more people when there are common values and visions that tie them together with others. Sure, there is great diversity among us, and that is the beauty of humankind. But just as surely as differences beautify, similarities unify!

When you review your values, culture, mission, and vision, look for places where the community links up with you. It can be as simple as your mission meeting a need of the people you want to reach. Wise leaders search for connection points, because this is where synergy is birthed. Where synergy comes alive, relationships find their genesis. For our ministry, the fourth tenet of our mission is that "We live to make a difference." We can easily connect with a community that needs some difference-makers to help out. We can easily connect with a community of people who want to be difference-makers.

Your job is to find the connection and emphasize it, not use the microscope of negative thinking to find every difference and magnify it. The more I look for common ground, the more I feel at home in my context. As I feel at home there, the more I believe I can make a difference there. Look for places to connect within your context.

WHO ARE THE MARGINALIZED?

"Marginalized" is a word we hear often, in a multitude of contexts. It's used for minorities, the poor, the sex-trafficked, etc., and those applications are appropriate. The word marginalized simply means people or people groups who are treated as insignificant or peripheral. They are not the mainstream. We don't think they truly count; the value of society seems not to be lessened by their loss.

There are several reasons to look for the marginalized in your context. First, I believe good things come to those who care about the "least of these." If nothing else, the sense of fulfillment that springs from kindness will improve both you and your leadership. Secondly, I believe that we often discover a deeper sense of purpose, vision, and mission when our hearts are open to those who have been made to feel insignificant. Finally, while your business may not cater to the marginalized, and your particular vision may not be for the so-called insignificant, many of the people you want to reach are tied directly or indirectly to these groups.

I encourage you to seek out the marginalized and find ways to provide for them. The greatest among us are not identified by what they have, but by what they are willing to give away. When your company appeals to the people with whom you want to connect, a door opens that can propel you towards success. Always remember that, in God's eyes, no one is peripheral.

THE POWER OF COLLABORATION

CHAPTER 4

BECOMING INTENTIONAL ABOUT PARTNERSHIPS

The second C in our exploration of key leadership principles is collaboration. Crisis teaches us that leadership is not a position; it is born from influence. We ascertain that leadership is not something to be grasped, but a difficult place where we serve those who need us most. In crisis, many of the resources we take for granted are in short supply. This predicament unlocks a potential power that existed before, but had not been nearly as critical: the power of collaboration—the ability to do things in connection with others that you could not have done by yourself.

Collaboration is defined as "the action of working with someone to produce or create something."[6] When organizations or individuals decide to collaborate, they mitigate the shortage of people, power, materials, or finances. I have discovered that, in crisis, the act of collaboration can move you from shortage to surplus in one fell swoop. Collaboration transitions us from the deficit of the individual to the surplus of the team, group, church, or business.

Collaboration during crisis normally happens because there is little choice. Still, the advantages are powerfully tangible. I encourage you to look for opportunities to connect with other leaders, teams, and organizations. There are latent possibilities hiding beneath the surface of our current separation—possibilities that are only released through authentic connection with others.

Collaboration driven by principle instead of need can create new opportunities for you and your organization. You and I find ourselves, at times, floundering as we long for more creativity, more brainpower, and more help. Rather than seeing yourself as a committee of one, see yourself as the person who creates a team and jettisons every member to a place of greater success. Individuals who pursue the formation of a team—before being forced to—have the confidence to unlock new potential in their organizations. When you consider how successful you've been on your own, consider the exponential growth that can happen when you add others to the process! The Bible states that while one can defeat a thousand, two can defeat ten thousand (see Deuteronomy 32:30). That math makes it worth your while to recruit some teammates!

When you connect with others, you create success for more people. This has tremendous rewards! Dave Ferguson and Warren Bird, in their book, *Hero Maker,* make the following claim: "When you invest in helping as many people as possible identify their unique calling and release them to pour into others, you exponentially increase *your impact.*"[7]

We increase our impact through the multiplication of teamwork, not merely the addition of more work for ourselves. In crisis, it seems that heroes arise out of the most unexpected places. This may be because crisis connects people who, normally, would have never found one another. It's not a strategy as much as an organic process that seems to be birthed by the need at hand. It was William Shakespeare who wrote, "Misery makes strange bedfellows." Crisis does the same. It puts people who never imagined working alongside one another in the same space.

Take the time to consider every project on your desk, your screen, your reminder list, and your phone. Then, ask yourself one question: "Who could help me with this?" Most of us will discover amazing new levels of productivity if we share only a *fraction* of our tasks with others. We will experience the joy of relationship we hadn't considered. We will know the satisfaction of not just being heroes, but "making heroes."

The intentional integration of others into your vision not only improves your level of productivity and enlarges your sphere of influence—it also enhances the lives of the individuals who join you. Too often, we forget that God's interest in our work is not primarily the work itself, but the pathway to completion and the lives we add value to along the way. You stand to touch as many people as the tasks you share with others. Whatever obstacles keep you from including others in the completion of your work can be overcome, because "help" can come in many forms.

- Ask people their opinion of what you're doing.
- Ask them to read what you have written and share their thoughts.
- Ask them if they have time to join your team.
- Ask if they have any shared experiences that might be helpful.

You may be thinking, "Everyone has enough work to do without having to help with mine!" Stop and think how you would feel if a colleague reached out and said, "I'm working on something. I know you've done this before, and you've done it well. Would you mind looking at what I have so far?" For those of us who live to add value to others, we get psyched when asked to contribute like this! Granted, there are some who will refuse to help, but that's their loss. They had the chance to join the ranks of the hero makers, and they missed it! That's not your issue. Simply keep your heart open to one of the most powerful tools I learned during crisis: the power of collaboration.

Cameron Randle was just a name on an email for a long time—until crisis changed that. Cameron was the rector of a local Episcopal church and a man who shared my heart for the marginalized and forgotten. Like me, he ran a successful food pantry out of his church that fed thousands every year. We never would have connected, but crisis hit. We would discover over time that the great need required us to marshal our collective resources and feed people together. Cameron moved from being a name on an email, to a voice on the phone, to a face on Zoom, to my brother and partner in ministry. Crisis taught me that I could get more done when I reached beyond my own small circle and connected with heroes—heroes who would not just help me, but *show me* how to be more effective in what I do.

TEAMWORK MAKES THE DREAM WORK

There is the dream of the work we do, and there is the pain we experience while doing that work. We seldom discuss (openly, at least) how completing our mission often leaves us wounded—maybe even a little frightened. For those who lead in times of war, casualties are anticipated—even expected. But peacetime warriors often lose sight of the true pain that our emotional battles bring. In times of crisis, we cry together more readily, we pray together more boldly, and we work together more organically. Somehow, when crisis ends, many go back to their secluded ways, their secret wounds, and their private pain. I have learned the power of teamwork to not only make dreams reality, but to stop nightmares.

John Ortberg said, "Never worry alone. When anxiety grabs my mind, it is self-perpetuating. Worrisome thoughts reproduce faster than rabbits, so one of the most powerful ways to stop the spiral of worry is simply to disclose my worry to a friend ..."[8]

We all have these moments—and if we're honest, we have them far more often than we let on. They highlight our human need for others to share our burdens. And, since we spend the lion's share of our waking hours working, what better place is there to experience teamwork?

Most of us use the word "team" daily. It's the new term for "staff," "team member," or "employee." While it is true that words can shape culture, "talking team" does not automatically make us one. In order for collaboration to extend from two or three working on a task together to teams accomplishing greatness, several things must happen.

ACCEPT the people on the team

Crisis teaches us not to be so choosy about who we choose. Our long list of required capabilities diminishes in times of trouble. Now, our mindset becomes, "Whoever is willing to join us is welcome. We can make it work!" Of course, I'm not implying you shouldn't do the important work of front-end onboarding when you select your team. I am saying that if the people are already there, and it's not your responsibility to remove or replace them, you need to accept them wholeheartedly.

SUPPORT the people on the team

Crisis turns every gathering into a support group. Levels of anxiety and fear are high. Even when we gather for work, the need to reassure one another prevails. As you lead or participate on a team—even one in which there is no imminent fear of death or disaster—remain sensitive to the needs of those working with you. Everyone needs to feel personal support from those with whom they spend significant amounts of time. This is no different. A sincere, "How are you today?" or an authentic, "I'm praying for you this week," can go a long way for a teammate who's down or discouraged.

BELIEVE in the people on the team

One of the first lessons you learn in a coaching class is how critical it is for people to feel that you believe in them. It might surprise you (or maybe it won't) to know the impact of simply saying, "I know you can do this." If I'm on your team and your tone and body language say that you *just know* I'm going to fail, it won't matter what your words say. Our belief in our teammates must come from an authentic place deep within. Thinking the best of others and encouraging them doesn't come naturally for many of us. But, like any discipline, time, practice, and awareness will change everything.

ENCOURAGE the people on the team

Much of this is elementary, but it's oftentimes the basics that bring us down. The simple act of consistent encouragement can change the destiny of a team. When supplies are low and danger and sickness abound, encouragement becomes the nourishment that keeps the soul and spirit going. You can encourage others one-on-one, in group settings, or both. Recently, during a personal crisis, a pastor friend's wife was diagnosed with cancer. I decided to encourage her daily. I didn't just hope I would remember—I made it a part of my scheduled, calendared appointments. When people are in tough places, they look forward to encouragement and are disappointed when it doesn't come.

Organizations, businesses, churches and individuals discover synergy they didn't know existed during times of crisis. It may be helpful for you to ask yourself a few leading questions:

What am I doing now that would have greater impact if I enlisted the help of others?

What am I planning to work on within the next year that would benefit from collaboration?

Within the last two years, have I decided against an undertaking—before considering collaborating with others—because we lacked the resources?

Do I have any teams that don't truly function as a team according to the four steps above? Where's the disconnect?

Does my organization have any activities that require the help of other organizations in order to be successful?

This simple assessment will help you begin to think outside of your personal or organizational "box" and open up a world of possibilities for you and others. Don't wait until crisis hits to catch the value of collaboration. If you started collaborating during a crisis, consider the advantages of continuing to do so long after the crisis has passed. You will add value to yourself, your team, your organization, and everyone you allow to work along with you.

CHAPTER 5

INCREASING ORGANIZATIONAL STRENGTH

As mentioned in the last chapter, the word collaboration means "the action of working with someone to produce or create something." It originated in the late 19th century from the Latin collaborat- which meant "work with" and came from the verb collaborare, from "col" ("together") and "laborare" ("to work").[9]

When we consider the etymology of the word that describes the power standard for automobiles, "horsepower" comes to mind. If one horse has a certain "horsepower," then two horses double that output. If you have enough power to get a task completed alone, you will *increase* your power when you connect with others. Collaboration increases strength and extends your reach. Co-laboring is what collaboration is all about. Teamwork multiplies your intellectual, emotional, academic, and material strength. Some may think of collaboration as a soft, subjective term with no real business value, but nothing could be farther from the truth.

When competition is not the fundamental concern, then collaboration is a key strategy for improving the position of both entities.

For most of us, competition isn't a fundamental concern in our business relationships. As the leader of a church, a nonprofit, and a for-profit business, I believe that making competition a key factor in relationships is a display of small-mindedness. If my church can't collaborate with other churches simply because more people may go to the other church, it speaks to my own insecurity! If my leadership network can't collaborate with another network to add value to lives, then what does that say about my leadership? If my consulting firm struggles to share ideas and dialogue with other firms, then what is my motivation for what I do?

Collaboration, on both the personal and the corporate level, exposes our fears and insecurities in a telling way. What's even more telling is examining how a company collaborates during crisis compared to how it collaborates when the crisis is over. If I'm willing to collaborate and receive help when *my* resources are low, but unwilling to help *others* when I'm doing fine, that says a lot about my motivations.

The power of a crisis is its ability to reveal how much we actually need one another. The truth is that we always need others, but prosperity is an effective mask that hides our deep dependence. During the recent crisis, I began getting regular calls from people whom I'd seldom heard from before trouble hit. Initially, I was suspicious; then, I realized that I, too, was reaching out more than I had previously. If the crisis had created a significant paradigm shift for me, then why would I doubt its ability to do the same in others? The authenticity of these kinds of shifts won't be revealed during the crisis—it only becomes apparent after things return to normal.

If you apply the principle of collaboration outside of crisis, it yields several advantages. First of all, there is less doubt about your motivations—you're not just reaching out to save your own skin. When you're not in crisis, you literally don't have to collaborate—instead, you're being proactive by choosing to do so. Secondly, what you employ during a non-crisis phase is more likely to continue in the long term than a hastily constructed collaborative strategy that comes about during crisis—one that, if we're honest, often leaves us reverting back to our old ways once the panic has passed. Thirdly, when you make collaboration a part of your normal process, you won't have to learn or relearn that skill when crisis arises. You will have already adjusted the culture of your organization and your own thinking to prepare for crisis. And, trust me: Crises will come more often than we think.

CEOS AND FOUNDERS

Let's talk through some of the challenges leaders face when they seek collaboration. As a founding leader, I understand the struggle of sharing what you've given your life to birth and maintain. Tom Mullins's discussion of succession is applicable to this conversation. He said, "Founders particularly fall into this category. When you start something, mature it, and enjoy the privilege of watching it grow, you will naturally feel a sense of loyalty and pride in it. This can make it really hard to step away and leave it in someone else's hands."[10]

The same is true for the leader wrestling with collaboration, especially if the area being considered is his or her "baby." All of us want to see continued success. However, as the leader, you set the pace for the rest of the team. If you aren't thrilled about collaborating, your team won't be either. The reverse is also true: If you become a proponent of working with others, your attitude will be contagious. Often, *you* hold the keys to cultural change in your hands. If you will turn the key in the lock, new ways of thinking—new opportunities—will be released!

MID-LEVEL MANAGERS/LEADERS

You may not be the CEO, the executive director, the senior or lead pastor, or the person who has the final say, but you are extremely influential! Whether you realize it or not, you are leading from the middle—influencing both the people who work for you and the people for whom you work. Don't underestimate the difference you can make in helping initiate the power of collaboration. While senior leaders make many decisions, the *execution* of those calls tends to be left in the hands of capable leaders like you. You have a leadership gift, strong relationships, and a plethora of connections both internally and externally.

When the CEO is uncertain, your experience, positive attitude, and track record can win him or her over. When the folks in the trenches are unsure about teaming up with the "other guys," you can be the encouraging voice they need. Who has the most to gain? You! Why? You can add one more success to your track record by extending your reach beyond where it's been in the past. You can prepare yourself for what many of us refer to as "real leadership"—the place where people follow you even though they don't have to do so! Seize the moment, and initiate collaboration during times of calm. Look for ways to include others who will double and triple your horsepower!

INDIVIDUAL CONTRIBUTORS

During my tenure in management with what was then known as Texas Instruments, I learned the term "individual contributor." This term was the company's way of valuing people who didn't have a staff to manage: analysts, financial experts, programmers, security personnel—great people who made major contributions to the company, but who weren't considered "management." You may be someone who doesn't feel that you're a leader because you lack a leadership title. As John C. Maxwell says, "Leadership is influence." If you have influence, you're a leader. And here's the thing: *Everyone* has influence. Your ability to employ principles of collaboration are infinite. Consider the task you're carrying out right now; whenever you reach out to a colleague for input, that's a measure of collaboration. Here are a few practical ways you can become a collaborator:

Research. When research is required, two heads are always better than one. You may not be the person who can decide to enter a collaborative relationship with an outside entity, but you can powerfully influence the internal collaboration that follows that decision.

Team Development. Unfortunately, many individual contributors tend to "go it alone." You can seek out opportunities to bring people together. That endless email trail that exists between people working 50 feet from each other is borderline ridiculous. You can be the person who says, "Hey, let's all meet in the conference room and do the unthinkable: *talk to each other*!" That's the power of collaboration.

Idea Development. Who better to lead a group of individual contributors in the process of developing new ideas than an individual contributor? You may have the opportunity to collaborate with another church, nonprofit, or business entity in facilitating new ideas that help all parties succeed. Still, if you can only collaborate internally, do it! You will be amazed at the level of division and intentional separation you can minimize within your own company.

ADDING VALUE IS RECIPROCAL

Our church owns a four-acre piece of property that used to be adjacent to an office building. Two decades ago, this office building was where we had to go to get our credit report. It was also the place to go if you happened to get turned down for credit. These offices existed in every city in the country. It's hard to believe that every single one of them is now obsolete! Because of the church's size, we cannibalized all the nearby parking: that of the mall across the street, the neighborhood behind us, our own lot, and that of this office complex. Once the building managers gave us permission to park in that lot on Sundays at no charge, we made a decision: Our staff would keep it clean Monday through Saturday, even when we weren't using it. This simple collaboration added value to both entities. We got much-needed parking space, and they had a maintenance-free parking lot for their staff.

Adding value to others is almost always reciprocated. It's a natural phenomenon. Collaboration during crisis has a clear "value added" result. The food bank has food, and we have a huge parking lot and volunteers. We get food to distribute, which helps us fulfill our mission to "make a difference." In turn, the food bank get its food distributed and fulfills its mission to "meet the needs of the food-insecure." Reciprocal value is added! During crisis, this happens easily because the needs are greater than either entity can handle alone. What made this reciprocal partnership with the food bank run so smoothly? We were already collaborating prior to any crisis.

When crisis hits, people immediately gravitate to collaborative relationships that are already in place.

The struggle, time, and energy spent in collaboration is well worth it when we consider the value added from those relationships. In some ways, collaboration is like other leadership principles. Let's take delegation for example. It takes a lot of work to delegate properly. Some say it's easier to simply do the work yourself than to "waste time" showing someone else who still won't do it as well as you! However, wise leaders know that spending that time provides them with someone who can easily take tasks from their plates and effectively handle them. It's ultimately worth the work! The same can be said for collaboration; it's hard work on the front end, but it yields amazing fruit on the back end. And the shelf life of collaboration is astounding.

By the way, I almost forgot to tell you the rest of the story about our office-building neighbors, whose parking lot we used and cleaned. When their business became obsolete, we collaborated again and purchased their property. Now, we park and work there every day. It's just one more proof that collaboration keeps adding value.

You can increase the functional strength of your personal work, your team, your church, or your company through collaboration. In the midst of crisis, it became inherently clear to me that entities with collaborative relationships were entrusted with more resources and given more authority to act and to lead. There is a reason for that—trust. Remember, when trust is high, change is easier and less costly. Collaborative leaders tend to be trusted leaders. People trust that they aren't merely in the collaborative relationship for themselves or for their organizations, because they have a track record of sharing work and credit. Additionally, collaborative leaders are more readily trusted because people have developed relationships with them prior to crisis.

You can strengthen your organization, add value, and earn the trust of others simply by working as a team player!

CHAPTER 6

THE ADDED VALUE OF COLLABORATION

Collaboration is made possible by accepting the value of another person or organization. Until I admit that someone has something I deem valuable, there can be no authentic collaboration.

Collaborative work that stems purely from emotional connections, empathy, or camaraderie is normally short-lived. Churches are famous for joint worship services or joint outreach—these partnerships happen because they feel it would be great to gather together—and it is. However, worshiping in the same space for a few weeks should not be confused with true collaboration. Collaboration is *working* together. Why do we need to drive this point home? Because otherwise, you'll be disappointed when what you thought was effective collaboration doesn't end up as successful as you envisioned.

Four years ago, my fellow MIT alum, Matt Breitenberg, asked if we could get together. Matt serves as the executive pastor of one of the leading churches in our region—a body that is predominantly Caucasian, evangelical, and an oasis of love, worship, and sound teaching. Matt shared that he and the lead teaching pastor, Eric Sanzone, had been praying about how to take steps toward eliminating the racism in their church. I was blown away by his candor and their vision. They asked if I would help by teaching in their church, and by bringing folks from our predominantly African American church together with their congregation for times of prayer. They didn't just want a joint worship service; they wanted the value in my ministry to be coupled with theirs in order to defeat racism. For four years now, we have worked together, and we've seen what the hard work of building relationships, stepping out of comfort zones, and valuing each other can accomplish.

This ongoing collaboration between the congregation of Grace Bible Fellowship and that of Calvary Revival Church (CRC) has been successful for several reasons, all of which emanate from the process of *identifying and applauding value*. These steps will be critical for you in your pursuit of collaboration. From the onset, there was a mutual expression of the other's value; everything we did rested on that. We weren't just a "Black church," and

Calvary wasn't just a "big church." Each body had specific qualities that would be essential in the battle against racism. Trust me, we all were in a crisis. Unarmed citizens were being killed regularly. Police officers were being ambushed. Churches were being attacked—and all in the name of racism. Christians were at a loss for what to do, but those at Grace decided to examine their hearts and change. The crisis helped them to conclude that we couldn't do this alone. We needed valuable, powerful partnership. And it just got better from there.

LOOK FOR EXISTING RELATIONSHIPS

Collaboration is much more likely to succeed when it involves existing relationships. A track record of trust becomes increasingly important as the level of risk increases. Eric had already begun to preach boldly about difficult topics like white privilege, racial profiling, and implicit bias. His church had been responding. Some were blessed by the conversation, and others would have no part of it. At this point, tapping a voice he knew to enter the conversation was a crucial step. Matt already knew me, and Eric had been tracking my ministry for some time. So when we met for coffee, there was no need to dance around introductions—we had an existing relationship.

Existing relationships reduce the time needed to complete a project, because the heavy lifting of figuring out motives has already been done. When you begin the work of collaboration, do your best to start with people you know—people who know you. It's not always possible, but when it is, go for it! Beginning with existing relationships provides a higher probability of success—and when you're at the onset, getting an early win only helps boost your confidence in the days ahead.

SEARCH FOR THE SPECIFIC STRENGTHS NEEDED

Grace Church needed a few specific things from its collaborative partner. It needed a partner that had an established reputation among diverse cultures and whose size was comparable to its size. The partner had to be made up of a different primary ethnicity but still hold shared values (which we will discuss in the next section). Every collaboration will have areas of need. Some are critical to success, while others may be preferences rather than needs. Clearly think through the areas that are needed in your organization that *you* are not able to supply; then seek out partners who meet those specific needs.

Once you've clearly defined your vision and mission and you know your destination, you can clearly map out the strategic steps required to get there. Too often, collaborative work is birthed and sustained by feelings instead of facts. Truthfully, if there are no clear strategic steps, progress is difficult to realize, let alone to sustain.

BUILD UPON SHARED VALUES

If eradicating racism wasn't important to me, our ministry wouldn't have made an effective partner for the other church. Even when you have an existing relationship and the strengths of both parties are evident, success is not likely unless there are shared values.

Shared values are not the same as core values. Most organizations list 3-5 core values—nonnegotiable items that provide the underpinning for the organization's culture, mission, and vision. Collaborative partnerships don't require you to have the same core values. If that were the case, not much collaboration would happen—in or out of crisis.

Shared values simply refer to the values that support your specific collaborative mission. Grace Church values helping believers live free from the sin of racism—being a church where people of all ethnicities are welcome. It values reaching out to everyone— independent of their color— in the community with needs. These may not be their core values, but they are important ones. When Grace reached out to ask if we would come alongside, the assumption was that we shared the same values. They were absolutely right: Nothing connected us more than how deeply we agreed with this value.

The recipe for relational disaster is two people or organizations who make a commitment to walk together yet do not care about the same things. Relationships can survive personality differences and even strategic differences, but they cannot survive differences in value.

CELEBRATE YOUR DIFFERENCES

As conflicting as it may seem, celebrating your differences in a collaborative relationship is as important as building on shared values. What gave real beauty to the collaborative work of our two churches? We valued the same thing, but we didn't look the same, worship the same, pray the same, or preach the same. We were not together *in spite* of our differences. We were together *because* of our differences. We loved worship time with the other church because it was so "sweet," and they loved praying with us because it was so "intense." Don't miss this when you start thinking about collaboration:

The reason you need each other to work together is not because you're alike but because you're different!

We didn't want the white members of Grace Church to feel they had to be "Black" any more than they wanted CRC people to be "White." We all wanted authenticity, because that's the source of success in every collaboration. I ask you to help me because you know something I don't; you're better at something than I am. You still have your strength in this space.

SET DEFINITIVE PLANS AND STRATEGIC STEPS

When we met to plan, we mapped out our strategy and next steps. We weren't the best at this part, but we never delegated much. There were three things we knew were important:

- Building relationships.
- Building a shared vision.

- Building corporate prayer.

Our plans began with an evening worship time that led to small group meetings all over the building. Stories were shared and email/phone numbers were exchanged. We knew that people have a difficult time getting past their biases until they hear someone else's story, so we sat in circles and answered questions and told one another about our life experiences.

Then, Eric and I sat in front of everyone and operated in our love for each other as we cast vision for a different church—a church that was not trapped in racism. We prayed and fasted together.

Collaborations, like everything else we do, have different time frames. Some will be completed in a few months; others, like the work with Grace, take years. We still have a long way to go, but we've seen progress, and we've built a relationship during crisis that has been maintained long after that particular crisis ended.

VALUE ADDED, VALUE RECEIVED

I cannot say enough about the intrinsic connection between understanding value and collaboration. Working together in a marriage, a ministry, or a major corporation are collaborations that are all built on the premise of value. Until you see the value you bring, the value they bring, and the value of your combined efforts, the chance of effective collaborative work is improbable.

How an individual or an organization assesses its own value plays a role in the ability to collaborate. The truth is that the insecurities which often keep people from working together stem from their poor views of their own value. If I can't work with you because I fear you may take my clients or my applause, that fear comes from not seeing my own value. If I'm driven by competition and the fear of losing, that's likely based on my own need to feel valued and be affirmed by winning. On the other hand, when leaders are confident in their giftings and abilities, they readily collaborate with others. They don't think of life in terms of "winning" and "losing," but in terms of adding value to others. Of course, the idea of adding value only makes sense if you know you *have* value to add in the first place.

The leader who collaborates with others must see the value in others, as well. This may seem obvious, but my refusal to work alongside others when there is a shared problem and shared values may be the result of not seeing the value *they* are bringing to the table. Granted, there will be times when the other organization simply can't add value to yours, but this should be the exception, not the rule. When you're thinking about working together in relationships, both personal and business, look for those you are sure will add value to you and your team.

Working together must ultimately bring about the greater good both for the organizations involved and for those they serve. Before you begin the collaborative process, I suggest that you ask yourself three questions:

- Do I bring something valuable to this process?
- Do I believe that the person/organization I'm working with brings value?
- Do I believe that, together, we will add value to the people we're attempting to serve?

In a crisis, there will always be someone in need of food, shelter, safety, or assistance. The decision to work together is generated by this need. We aren't working together for appearances or promotions. We are working together for the common good. I bring value, you bring value, and our combined value reshapes the situation we face. Our resources and ideas will meet a critical need in our community. If you're in crisis, look for the chance to work together with others. If there is no crisis, *still* look for the opportunity to work together for the good of others.

The result? You will add value to the people with whom you work. The people you work with will add value to you. And, the value you bring together will be the answer that many are searching for.

THE POWER OF COMMUNICATION

CHAPTER 7

THE COMMUNICATION PROCESS

Next up on our list of Cs is one we talk about often, but don't employ effectively nearly enough! Communication is one of the most overused words in our vocabulary, but the *act* of communication is one of our least consistent practices!

We spend a lot of time talking about communicating, but we don't seem to do communication very well. It reminds me of Christians who use the words "pray" or "prayer" ten times as often as they actually pray. There's a reason why some terms are used frequently but not practiced consistently, and it's a result of the disconnect between the heart and the mind.

In our hearts, we know we need to pray—to communicate with God—but our minds lower the priority of prayer until it becomes something many of us do only when we become desperate. Communication with others tends to follow the same pattern, based on a similar disconnect. Our hearts know very well how important it is to communicate thoughts and actions with others. Our minds...not so much.

Tim LaHaye once quipped, "Communication is to relationships what blood is to the body!" Somehow our minds lower the need to communicate to a level of priority in which we only do it when absolutely necessary...Enter crisis. During crisis, my communication skills grew exponentially. I'm not implying that I became a better communicator, but I did start communicating more frequently. The pressure of the crisis forced my mind and its priorities into agreement with what my heart had always known.

If we can capture some of the lessons learned and habits forged during crisis in this critical area of communication, we can improve efficiency and effectiveness as leaders.

COMMUNICATE IN CONTEXT

Normally, the discussion about communication begins with the message; however, crisis has taught me that my message is not as important as understanding *whom* my message is for. My message may change, but my target does not. In fact, knowing my audience better may actually adjust my message. So, we'll start by discussing the process of determining your audience.

When COVID-19 began, I was immediately concerned about the food-insecure of our communities. In haste, I began to develop a communication strategy that was social media-driven. As I thought about my audience, I realized that this might not be the best strategy. The elderly were more likely to be stuck at home with no food, and more susceptible to the long-term negative impacts of the virus. My audience wasn't all on social media. Radio, television, personal calls, and written communication might have been more effective than social media for them.

When we're leading in crisis, we have a specific problem we are attempting to solve. Our leadership is extremely pragmatic because crisis calls for rapid action, not the appearance of cool. We immediately start thinking about the best practices for reaching our audiences; there is so much at stake. How do we ensure the same commitment to our communication process when there is no crisis?

THE ISSUE MAY NOT BE A CRISIS...FOR YOU

Not every issue we set out to solve is a crisis for everyone. It may not be a *global* crisis. It may not be a *pan*demic. However, to the person in need, it is a crisis nonetheless. Once we begin to understand our context and collaborate with others to develop solutions, we must communicate as if lives depend on it. They often do.

No matter how life-changing your message, it won't matter if it doesn't reach the ear of the person for whom it's meant. No one wants to waste time barking up the proverbial wrong tree.

Once you begin to establish a sense of urgency, you're in a good place to begin thinking about your message itself. In most cases, there are several layers to the message. We need to research, in order to be sure we fully understand the problem we're seeking to address. This will require us to communicate in a series of questions or to conduct surveys.

We also need to communicate a heart to serve. Our audiences and those we serve need to know our motives and our hearts to meet their needs. We must communicate with our collaborative partners and tell the people how to access our solutions. Of course, this is more complicated than is needed for some scenarios, but there is no such thing as overcommunicating!

INTERNAL COMMUNICATION

Believe it or not, the place where communication processes most often break down is internally. We tend to take internal communications for granted, which opens up the door for failed interaction after failed interaction. Here are a few simple guidelines you need to follow as you develop your communication process:

1. Determine the effectiveness of your regular team or staff meetings.

- Do meetings happen as consistently as planned?
- Is there an established, ongoing approach to discussion *between* meetings?

- Do all feel their voices are heard. Do all have equal access to decision-makers?
- Is there effective follow-up on action items?

2. Determine the effectiveness of your digital messaging.

- How accurate and up-to-date is your website?
- How accurate and up-to-date is your company's app?
- Do you have a current strategy in place for the use of social media?

3. Determine your communication effectiveness as the leader.

- How often do you meet with team members individually?
- How often do you meet with your team as a whole?

4. Determine the clarity of your organization's mission.

- How clear and simple is your vision/mission?
- Does your organization know and understand your vision?
- How much does your mission actually impact your actions, decisions, and events?
- Your willingness to not only answer these questions honestly but also to ask your team to weigh in will revolutionize the communication of your organization.

WHO DOES THE TALKING?

Leading in crisis has taught me that, sometimes, the messenger is more important than the message. Interestingly, people often hear the heart of a leader or spokesperson louder than they hear the message. This is why choosing who will speak for you is an important call. There are several factors that go into this decision.

The person speaking for your team or organization needs to have a good track record. We've discussed the power of trust, and that it is intrinsically tied to change. Leadership is, in most cases, moving people from point A to point B. When the communicator has a strong track record, he or she also gains the trust of your audience much more easily. The right person to speak is not always the person in charge or the most articulate. Look for that positive history.

The person who speaks for you must possess an empathy that can be felt by your audience. Empathy can be defined as, "the ability to understand and share the feelings of another."[11] Some people have it, and others don't, but empathy can't be taught or given. If you have empathy, you *can* be taught how to better express it, but you have to possess it in the first place.

Whatever your message may be, and to whomever it's spoken, empathy is critical. It really is true in almost every case: *People don't care how much you know until they know how much you care!* Whether the communication is with your staff, the teams collaborating, or the communities you're serving, empathy will be a game changer.

COMMUNICATION IS CRITICAL TO COLLABORATION

As we discussed in the section on collaboration, your ability to communicate makes every other part of your efforts that much more powerful. When multiple people, teams, or business entities begin to collaborate, the need to communicate well goes up—as well as the risk we take if we *fail* to communicate.

For example, if there is a clear message to share in a collaborative setting, there are at least two independent entities or teams that are involved in sharing that message. There must be strong internal communication. The parties collaborating must ensure that they agree on the message as well as how and when to share it. (Chapter 9 will talk about communication strategy in detail.) Additionally, a long-term communication process must be in place so that the message remains intact and the relationship between the collaborative partners remains solvent.

COMMUNICATE TO CREATE

It's unfortunate that some leaders only communicate in order to put people in check, correct them, or share difficult information. For some, a communication strategy is merely something to use when you have bad news to share, and you want to minimize the damage. But your voice was designed to strengthen, build up, and create—not to tear down. Let's talk through some ideas that will keep your communication both positive and powerful.

Always prepare before communicating. Never speak publicly "off the cuff." When possible, write out your thoughts, organize them, and set a time limit for yourself.

Always identify what you want your audience to remember after you present. Determine 2-3 of these takeaways, and make sure you "nail" those points in your address.

Always be clear on who your audience is before addressing it. My worst presentations happened not because of bad content, but because I failed to understand to whom I was talking as I prepared the message.

Always think about how your words are adding value. There are facts to share, and all facts may not be pleasant, but as a leader, you need to find a way to build up your audience even when the news you have to share is difficult.

COMMUNICATE TO CELEBRATE

Leaders communicate internally with staff and teams, as well as externally with collaborative partners and the communities they serve. However, we sometimes forget a significant communication responsibility of leaders: vision-casting. It's your responsibility to communicate what the future holds and how your people must prepare for and perform in the next season. Leaders share data from past performance and use it to provide the perspective needed to be effective. At the same time, we can't forget to communicate for the purpose of *celebration*! In order to inspire the people that make the dream a reality, we must learn to recognize every win—to rejoice over every victory. In crisis, you learn the importance of morale and, by extension, the importance of every acknowledged victory.

Your challenges are many, your problems seem insurmountable, and your losses are discouraging. When you find a win in the midst of this atmosphere, you have to mention it. The same can be said for times outside of crisis—remember, it may not be a crisis to you, but it is to someone. The need to celebrate transcends pandemic, war, and natural disaster. In those moments between crises, the effective leader *still* finds something to celebrate. When you don't reach the goal, celebrate the effort; when sales revenue is less than expected, celebrate the improvements. When someone gives their all and, for reasons outside of their control, it doesn't work out, celebrate their efforts. Every time you do this, you're simultaneously casting vision.

COMMUNICATE VISION AND EXECUTION

Leading in crisis teaches us what works (and doesn't work) in communication. A one-sided communication that shares vision in an abstract way is good, but without an execution plan, it won't get you very far. On the flip side, if we only talk about how we plan to fund and execute the vision but never touch people's souls, then we won't have the inspiration we need.

In *New Thinking, New Future,* Dr. Sam Chand gives us great advice: "Leaders need to be bilingual. They have to communicate in the abstract language of vision and they have to speak the concrete language of execution." In crisis, people are anxious and petrified about what the future holds.

If they only hear about the logistics of executing vision, they will lack the inspiration to carry out the vision—*even if they agree with it!* However, people in crisis need concrete facts as well, so they can face the truth and plan for it. It's all about balancing these two aspects of vision.

This places you as the vision-caster in a somewhat precarious position. You still have the power and the opportunity to get results—if you make the effort to become "bilingual." Think about the vision in your heart, and ask yourself two questions: "What do I need to share to provide people with understanding, inspiration, and comfort?" and "What do I need to share to give people the facts they need about how we will execute this?" You will, essentially, answer the two most important questions: "Why?" and "How?" If you do this, it will give your people both the inspiration and the information they need to fulfill your great vision.

CHAPTER 8

EFFECTIVE COMMUNICATION

We use the word "communication" a great deal; however, the term is often misused. Some leaders believe that being articulate makes you a great communicator, while others believe that writing skills are the true indication of a strong communicator. Based on the definition of communication, these presuppositions are not true. While some great speakers are great communicators and many powerful authors are good communicators, one does not necessarily determine the other.

Communication is defined as "the successful imparting or exchanging of information and/or news."[12] Therefore, while some people may speak or write well, if their information is not imparted or exchanged successfully, then no communication has actually taken place. Talking is *not* communication; neither are writing, endless meetings, or persistent texts or emails. Communication and community come from the same root word that means "exchange." It takes place when information goes out *and* comes in.

Leading in crisis has taught me the truth about communication. After all, crisis requires that information be exchanged successfully—lives are often hanging in the balance. There is so much more at stake during these times than sounding brilliant or impressive. Let's take a look at how to move towards truly effective communication.

CLEAR. CONCISE. CASCADING.

One of my mentors says good communication is **clear**, **concise** and **cascading**.[13] What does that mean? Here's how I interpret these principles:

Clear communication from a leader is vital. In crisis, one of the greatest needs people have is to find peace in the midst of the challenge. And while every crisis is not a pandemic, terrorism, or war, people may still feel the pressures of their own personal crises. Whether it's a global crisis or a personal one, everyone needs clarity in order to establish peace. The Greek New Testament word for "peace" has nothing to do with the absence of trouble. Instead, it means "to be reconciled." In faith, this refers to reconciliation to God, but there is a more general meaning, as well.

Peace and reconciliation are synonymous in ancient languages because peace comes when you reconcile certain things to be true and trustworthy regardless of what you see in reality. When we communicate in a clear way, it produces peace—now, people can reconcile, or connect, their thinking, their words, and their actions with clear truth. Clear communication removes the guesswork and annihilates confusion. The result is peace. No matter with whom you're exchanging information, make certain you're crystal clear. There is nothing wrong in asking those with whom you've shared the question, "Was I clear?" Just be prepared to adjust your strategy if their facial expressions say, "Not really!"

Conciseness is the skilled communicator's best friend. Many of us have heard the acronym KISS: Keep It Simple, Stupid! Alternatively, Keep It Short! I've often commented that the worst speakers seem to be the longest-winded ones! Why? Somehow, they think they'll find their voice, figure out their thoughts, or happen upon a clear theme if they just keep going. But it never happens; it just gets worse. It can be assumed in most cases that a lack of conciseness is the result of two things: an unprepared message and/or an unprepared messenger. Very often, the two go hand in hand. Unless you're conducting a physics lecture, anything you share should be concise. And, when you can't do this, go back and look at a few things in your content:

Do I know what I want to say? Have you determined the 1-2 things you want your audience to know when you're done?

Do I believe in what I'm saying? It's difficult to be concise when you're not sure if you're fully committed to what you're communicating. Trust me: Your audience will see, feel, and hear the sound of uncertainty!

Do I know what I'm talking about? Too often, leaders begin a discussion without being fully prepared. While you're not expected to be the expert regarding every topic, people do expect you to be the expert on the topics on which you communicate. If you're not, then the expert should be in the room with you. If I've learned anything from crisis communication, I have learned this: When you're not the expert and the expert is with you, for goodness' sake, *shut up and let the expert talk!*

Lastly, communication needs to be **cascading**. We'll spend more time discussing this in the chapter on communication strategy, but let's explore the principle here just a bit. "Cascading" simply means "flowing at certain levels." Waterfalls cascade down, with the flow beginning at the top and rolling majestically down a mountainside. When you're preparing to communicate to any group of people, make sure you answer this question: "Who needs to hear this *first?*" What we learn in crisis is powerful, because appearance is not as important as practicality.

During a time of crisis, if I don't tell the right people first, the results could be catastrophic. Many leaders have learned the hard way that this lapse in communication ends in setback for your team or organization. So develop a plan to communicate a clear plan to Level 1 leaders, then Level 2 leaders, and so on and so forth. You don't want the folks most critical to the process finding out last. My moment of greatest perceived communication failure is when my wife says, "Oh, I didn't know we were doing that until I heard the announcement at church." And the funeral music plays...

Clear. Concise. Cascading. All of these are essential to your communication.

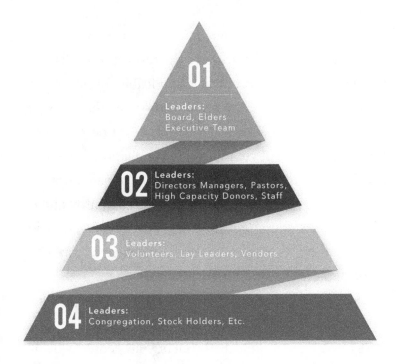

Let's take this a step farther and lay out a simple template for how you will share your message. I learned this from Martin van Tilborgh, and I call it "Triple A."

A: Acknowledge the Facts

Leaders often wrestle with this part of the communication process. They think, "I don't want to discourage them. I don't want to hurt morale." Can I tell you something? Morale will be hurt even more if you don't tell people the truth. You'll only have to come back later and correct your mistake. The facts are what they are and, whether you share them or not, they will eventually surface. You might as well be honest up front.

As the trusted leader, you are the best person to share the facts, because you already have the respect of your hearers. Once again, Covey's premise is applicable: In order to lead people through change, there must be trust that minimizes the pain of the process. You're also the best person to share the facts because of your intimate connection to your audience. This relationship softens the blow of bad news, partly because you tend to communicate with empathy and concern. Because communication is primarily nonverbal, leaders have the opportunity to send a message of care simply through their tone and body language.

The bottom line is this: Trust the ability of the people you lead to understand, handle, and apply the facts appropriately. If you will communicate the facts, your people will appreciate you for keeping them informed.

A: Acknowledge the Questions

I remember so many times after I had finished speaking when people wanted to ask me follow-up questions. I thought, "If I let them ask questions, it will never end." I feared questions, even though I was relatively good at answering on the fly—even though I had adequate knowledge of my material. For a long time, I thought that questioning a leader was a sign that the leader wasn't being honored or trusted. In my latter years, I've discovered that, very often, the opposite is true—questioning is more often a sign of sincere interest. This newfound understanding has completely changed my attitude toward question-and-answer time. Now, I look forward to answering people's follow-ups.

Make it clear when you communicate that you welcome questions and will do your best to answer them. If you don't know the answer, be committed to finding it—and again, be honest with your audience.

A: Ask for Support

Asking the people with whom you communicate to support you is a healthy practice to begin doing right now—whether you're in crisis or not. Both unity and ownership are increased when we freely solicit one another's help. Your team, your staff, and your organization will increase its synchronicity when you share your own need for support. It will also give your followers permission to do the same with one another!

If you can remember the three Cs of communication—clear, concise, and cascading—they will provide a valuable framework for you to use as you're preparing to exchange information. Likewise, the Triple A acronym provides you with guidance on the actual content of your communication. Acknowledge the facts and the questions, and ask for continuing support.

Finally, let's talk about your focus when communicating—more specifically, *on whom* you focus. As the saying goes, "One size doesn't fit all." You need to customize your communication plan. The following principles will help you do just that, based on who is listening to your message.

INTERNAL COMMUNICATION

You need to communicate well with your team and your organization. Don't minimize the power of internal communication. Crisis has taught me that chaos doesn't remove the need to share vision with those on my team. There are several specifics that must be shared and shared again on an internal level.

Vision/Mission

Your mission and vision must be shared clearly, and you must help those on your team see the connection between the vision/mission and your current endeavors. Vision and mission connect the team around one theme, and a common vocabulary creates a culture that can conquer any obstacle. If you're considering collaboration with other organizations, it's critical that your organization understands its *own* purpose before linking up with outside help. This understanding of purpose will help your team more readily connect with other organizations, while keeping high morale and unity internally.

Staff Significance

Paid staff is critical to the execution of any vision or mission. Pastor Matthew Watley said, "An organization is only as good as its staff, and if staff isn't connected to vision, there's no chance for organizational success."

It's critical to communicate to staff how important they are, as well as your organization's commitment to them, both short term and long term. During a recent crisis, when most hourly people were losing their jobs, we fought to keep every one of our hourly employees. We wanted to communicate their value to them—to assure them that they truly did matter. We'd already spent three years communicating value through staff retreats, training for their personal development, and added benefits. This was just another step in that process.

Our efforts have resulted in increased attendance and giving, and our highest volunteer involvement ever in the history of our church!

EXTERNAL COMMUNICATION

Communicating with those outside of your organization is simultaneously similar *and* different from your internal communication. Those outside your organization require a different type of communication: They need to know your heart towards others as well as your values.

Core Values

Look for engaging ways to share with your customers, clients, and collaborative partners the values that frame your organization—the reasons you do what you do. Core values such as serving, loving others, and giving speak volumes to those outside your organization. The community at large needs to know your values and be able to relate to them.

Mission

Every facet of our mission is important to our organization, but not necessarily to those outside of the organization. For example, our mission is that we exist to help people know God, live generously, discover purpose, and make a difference. While the first three may not seem applicable to outsiders, the final tenet always gets their attention. We want to *make a difference*. Everyone we work with feels connected to this part of our mission. People in our communities want to make a difference, and they want to connect with people who are pursuing the same thing.

Donors

If you're connected to a group of donors, this is another area in which strong external communication must be employed. The more time you spend interacting with high-capacity donors, the more connected they'll feel with your vision. A clear, concise vision for the future inspires givers and keeps them investing into your purpose. Regularly reach out by email, phone, or conference call to communicate this.

All of this information needs to be planned out well. This is what has come to be known as your *communication strategy*, and the next chapter will teach you how to craft and refine yours.

CHAPTER 9

DEVELOPING A COMMUNICATION PLAN

For many years, I led my organization without producing a communication strategy. My first time hearing about the importance of a strategy was when I spoke with my director of marketing. We were involved in a frivolous lawsuit against a member of our staff that was eventually thrown out of court by the judge. My director of marketing instructed me to write down, verbatim, everything I was going to say in response to this situation. As I would come to learn, this communication strategy would assist me in staying on script, speaking to the right people, and speaking at the right time.

Although this particular communication strategy was predicated by "negative" news, the use of a strategy isn't reserved for this kind of message. When positive news is shared, there still exists a need to develop a strategy. Why? When information is communicated to the people you influence, timing and content are *everything*. Your strategy helps you to place the conversation—not simply to let it happen spontaneously. Consider how many times you've been a little nervous and forgotten one of the "three things" you want to share. Nerves, crowds, deadlines, and emotions can all create stress that shuts the brain down. A communication strategy helps you to say the right thing—and, because it minimizes stress, it helps you say things in the right way.

The most critical advantage of a communication strategy, in my opinion, is the opportunity to follow a schedule. When there's no schedule for communication, people can find things out too early or too late. When we fail to plan out the timeline, people get a chance to create their own narratives before we're able to share ours. When I relieve someone of a position in which that person supervises several other people, here's my normal plan: I sit down with the person and release him or her to the person's new ministry. However, I don't have that person share with the team yet. Instead, I go with the person to meet with the team and share the good news. No one gets to create a personal narrative, because I'm present throughout the process. Everyone stays on the same page about the change. This is the effectiveness of a communication strategy.

WHEN IS A COMMUNICATION STRATEGY NEEDED?

As I mentioned earlier, leaders often think communication strategies are for communicating bad news. I disagree. Anytime a leader has important information to be shared with a group or groups—whether inside or outside of the organization—there needs to be a well-thought-out plan.

Think about what's important and what's unimportant—what's significant and what's insignificant. How do you decide these things? Think about it from the perspective of your hearers. As a leader, it may seem trivial to you, but it might be the most important thing to your audience. Ask yourself the following questions:

Is this information critical to the fulfillment of our vision and mission?

Some information can be emailed to staff and volunteers, because it's logistical or celebratory—there is no need for a complex strategy. However, when information challenges your mission, vision, and values, then you should consider a communication plan in order to deliver it in a clear, intentional manner.

Will this information help our morale if shared properly?

Announcements about restructuring or reorganization, if shared wisely, can bring excitement and even relief to your audience. Be keenly aware of those exchanges that have the potential to lift everyone's hearts and clear their minds.

Could this information hurt our morale if shared improperly?

Some information may not be extremely critical in and of itself; however, if it's mishandled, it could tank morale and discourage your team. For example, let's say you have a long-time staff member who is retiring, and everyone already knows who will take that person's place. Rumors have been floating around that the retiree was forced out because his or her performance was lackluster. This is not wildly significant in itself, but if it was miscommunicated, there could be repercussions. If shared improperly, this could have an adverse effect in your organization. Be aware of information like this, and handle it appropriately.

Does the timing of sharing this information matter?

Some announcements have timing ramifications. They need to be shared prior to an event or a change in the organization. If the timing is mishandled, it will create issues for your organization. Whenever timing could be a problem, set up a plan or timeline with specific steps.

Does it matter with whom I share this information?

When there is information that must be shared with specific people or groups of people, a communication plan is needed. If there is more than one group with which you intend to communicate, it's important to develop a strategy that takes into account the exact time that each group will meet.

In keeping with Sam Chand's theory of cascading communication, here is an example of a recent communication plan at our church:

We were in the process of changing our logo and updating our mission statement. We started by meeting with our governing board in the morning, all leadership teams by lunchtime, staff in the afternoon, lay leaders at 6pm, volunteers at 7pm, and the church at 8pm. I felt tired by the end of the day, but this cascading communication resulted in increased excitement with every session. Powerful things can happen, and an entire organization can take off, when a communication strategy is developed and executed properly.

THE STEPS TO YOUR COMMUNICATION PLAN

The first step to crafting your communication plan is to think of what you want to accomplish in the process. What's the message you want each person, or group, to receive? What's your goal?

Be as detailed as you possibly can in developing your message. Leave nothing to the imagination. Review it to be sure it truly says what you want people to hear, and be aware that, while it may seem clear to *you*, it may not be as straightforward to your audience. Take time to practice with a couple of trusted people, and get honest feedback from them.

As we discussed previously, determine which groups will hear your message first, second, and so on. This will help you develop a schedule for your strategy. In many cases, top-level people have more flexibility than the final, larger group you meet with, so you may want to start by determining when your larger group can meet and work backwards in order to establish times. For example, if I need to complete my strategy by sharing with a few thousand people at church, then I need to determine when I can get in front of that group; then, I can work backwards to scheduling times to meet with volunteers, staff, leaders, and board members.

Once you have your scheduled times, determine exactly where you will meet with these groups and for how long. Determine how much time you will need for questions and answers, as well. Make sure to address every possible detail in your planning—the more you can write out, the fewer surprises you'll have, and the smoother the process will ultimately be.

SEVEN POWERFUL IDEAS TO BOOST YOUR COMMUNICATION STRATEGY

In *New Thinking, New Future,* Sam Chand outlines powerful steps for communicating vision. They are adapted here to help you prepare your message once you have your strategy.

Chase the Dream

You may have a specific message to share, but remember that nothing we envision is static! Give people the sense that, in agreeing with you, they are chasing something bigger than themselves. Give wings to everyone who hears you!

Cultivate the Concept

Make sure you've spent the time to cultivate the various concepts in your message. This can be done by celebrating wins and celebrating the people in the room who have made those victories possible. Be prepared to keep encouraging people even after you share the message. Cultivate before, during, and after!

Cut the Crowd

Not everyone is going to get excited about every message you communicate. It's essential to know which ones *are* excited, and get those people front and center when you make your announcement. This will help you stay upbeat and will ultimately impact the entire room.

Cast the Net

There will be people in the room who are all in—people you never expected to be on board! Note these individuals in your mind, and write their names down the first chance you get. Reach out to them, and make sure they have an opportunity to connect with this segment of the vision.

Commit to Consistency

Remain committed to the next steps you outline *after* you have communicated your message. We all know that obstacles will arise, but you have the power to see your vision all the way through. If you aren't committed, neither will your people be.

Connect the Dots

Great leaders help people to see how one area of vision connects to another. Connect departments, connect people, and connect resources. Connecting these dots also requires repetition—saying the same things over and over. People forget; they get distracted. Sometimes, the message just doesn't click. Keep talking, keep repeating, and stay patient as you work to connect the dots.

Care for the People

My pastor, Richard Hilton, always says, "Jesus was never interested in crowds—He was interested in people!" Leaders who care for individuals will inevitably attract the people they need to fulfill their vision. When you're working on your communication strategy, keep the faces of your people in front of you at all times. Richard always reminded me, "It's people before things!" Every message you strategize to communicate must include the desire to *add value* to people—no matter what.

If people are our highest priority, our service will naturally improve, and the resources we need will come.

Follow-Up Steps

After you've executed your communication strategy, you have some options to choose from in following up with your hearers.

PERSONAL FEEDBACK

Choose 2-3 people from each group, and either sit down with them personally or email them as a group. Ask these people a few questions that will indicate how well they received your message. If you shared a message detailing a new endeavor for your organization, you might choose to ask them what they see as the primary strength of the new endeavor. Then, you might ask how each sees his or her role in it. Be sure to ask open-ended questions, like a coach would use. You don't want "Yes" or "No"—you want to hear how your message impacted their hearts. Logistics can always be learned later on, but it's the "Why" that moves people to act.

TEAM FEEDBACK

Meet with some of your leadership teams, and ask for their thoughts on the message. Ask them how, as leaders, they can support that message. Your follow up, and the feedback you collect, should serve to connect people to the vision and mission in an authentic way.

Next Steps

During times of sharing your message, always close with these 3-4 steps so that, after people hear your message, they know what to expect. These next steps also provide a powerful framework for follow-up.

Crisis leadership is not for the faint of heart! Crisis discovers and deploys real leaders—people who lead without titles and are followed by those whose checks they don't sign. You haven't functioned effectively as a leader until someone is following you who doesn't have to do so! When you're working on your communication strategy, remember that you need people to follow you to a specific place. Reach out for their hearts, and they will give you their hands, their treasures, and their talents.

THE POWER OF CONTINGENCY

CHAPTER 10

WHEN THE FIRST PLAN DOESN'T WORK

The last C we're going to look at is contingency. Proverbs 19:21 says, "You can make many plans, but the Lord's purpose will prevail." When the writer of Proverbs penned this statement, it was likely in the face of some outlying contingencies. The outcomes of war, famine, or personal attack can all be considered contingencies. This word is simply defined as "dependence on chance or on the fulfillment of a condition; uncertainty; fortuitousness."[14]

There are things happening which we can plan on with relative certainty, but there are also events that could *possibly* occur. It's for the latter type of occurrence that we need contingency thinking. The wise saying above clearly states, "You can make many plans!" While there is a singular purpose or plan of God that will ultimately prevail (Theologians call this the sovereignty of God.), we don't always know what that ultimate sovereign result will be. Wisdom teaches us that the smartest thing we can do is to have more than one plan! After all, most of the time our plans and God's plans are not one and the same.

Crisis teaches us a similar lesson. Leading in the midst of catastrophe is extremely pragmatic; it forces us to plan for all the possibilities. In our recent crisis, as we faced a global pandemic, people were hungry, impoverished, and sick. We couldn't simply plan for what we'd do if the pandemic lifted in 30 days. No—we had to have contingency thinking—to plan for 90 days, 120 days, or longer. This isn't a lack of faith; it's an admission that we are not God and cannot with total accuracy predict the future. *Our* plans must be plural, knowing that *the Lord's* plan will ultimately prevail.

While the notion is true that we do "hope for the best and plan for the worst," contingency thinking isn't merely a means of addressing the negative. This kind of strategizing also takes into account our hopes and the good things that could happen. "If sales double...if donations increase by 25%...if attendance goes up by 100..." These are also contingencies. Our plans must be full-scope, including both negative contingencies and positive ones.

Contingency thinking must proceed contingency planning!

It can be said that the difference between good leadership and great leadership is the ability to be ready for what an uncertain future may hold. Greatness is the result of building in enough robustness—enough strength—to handle the contingencies of life. In my leadership journey, I've found that it has been the things I failed to plan for that have most impeded my progress. The old saying, "A failure to plan is a plan to fail," is accurate. Some people might lead us to think that planning is a show of doubt, but the wise words of Jesus tell us otherwise:

> *For which one of you, when he wants to build a tower, does not first sit down and calculate the cost to see if he has enough to complete it? Otherwise, when he has laid a foundation and is not able to finish, all who observe it begin to ridicule him.* —Luke 14:28-29 (NASB)

CONTINGENCY PLANNING

A contingency plan is not synonymous with a fallback plan. A fallback plan is what you create when an existing plan fails. A contingency plan, on the other hand, is what you create when a calculated risk in the future becomes a reality. For example, you know it's possible that your home could catch on fire. You'll want to create a contingency plan for getting your family out of the house as quickly as possible. If the contingency plan fails, then you'd rely on a fallback plan.

A contingency plan is a course of action designed to help an organization respond effectively to a significant future event or situation that may or may not happen. It's sometimes referred to as "Plan B," because it can be used as an alternative if the expected results fail to materialize.

Sometimes, success reflects the number of calculated risks we're willing to take—both personally and professionally. This is why contingency planning is so important: It allows for active risk management and proactive preparation, instead of reactive decision-making in the face of an emergency, which more often than not results in failure. Contingency thinking is key to long-term success in that the ability to plan for calculated risks is essential to an organization's future.

Before our recent crisis, we had completed our annual budget and predicted a slight increase in revenue; still, we kept our spending flat or slightly reduced. When the pandemic hit, we had to roll out a different plan. If revenue falls based on our inability to have weekly services, then our existing budget quickly becomes invalid—thus the need for a contingency budget that assumes the calculated risk of a revenue fall of 25-30% based on the level of electronic giving at the time. We made the huge assumption that those who were giving electronically would continue to give.

We were also feeding people in our food-distribution ministry every week; normally, around 150-200 families weekly would come through. Here's an example of multiple contingencies we considered related to food distribution as a result of the pandemic:

- What if we are no longer able to allow people inside the distribution center?

- What if the needs increase significantly?
- What if our inventory is not adequate for the needs?

The questions forced us to totally revamp how we've handled food distribution. We drew up the following points in our contingency plan:

1. If we cannot serve inside, we will serve in the parking lot.

2. If the need increases significantly, we will set up drive-through stations and multiple lanes.

3. If we run out of food, we will leverage relationships with the food bank and with grocery stores.

Trust me, my friend—we had to do all three! The needs more than quadrupled over a three-week period. Contingency thinking allowed us to keep serving in spite of the risks.

These examples come from days of great crisis, but a template can be created to be utilized even in the absence of a crisis.

Scott Leshinski asks the following three questions that I think may help us frame our contingency thinking/planning template:[15]

Can your organization accurately model "what-if" scenarios to analyze the depth and duration of disruption and quantify the financial impact on your business? Based on the range of scenarios, can you quantify the impact on your liquidity needs, capital structure needs and cash burn? Have you prepared a series of contingency plans to address any financial, operational and cash flow issues for all potential scenarios?

Here's a practical framework to use as you begin your contingency planning process:

What are the "what ifs" in my organization today?

The ability to accurately model "what if's" simply means this: You can map out in detail what these situations could possibly look like. "What if's" are the known uncertainties you face. This is not you thinking of every negative thing that could happen in your organization, but rather a way to ensure you've addressed the obvious issues that could arise and create catastrophic circumstances.

What if your top leader leaves or dies? What if your building burns to the ground? What if the number of people attending your services surpasses your seating capacity? What if you run out of small groups? What if your current primary vendor goes out of business? These are just some ideas to get you thinking.

Can I determine the financial impact of these "what ifs"?

This is a critical step in the thinking process, because it requires your team to quantify your potential calculated risks. Look at the "what if" examples in the previous paragraph, and began to put dollar figures next to them. Having a plan doesn't mean there won't be a cost if the calculated risk becomes a reality.

Here's an example: If your top leader dies, you may have the contingency plan of succession and even a key man policy (an insurance policy taken out on the primary leader and, upon his death, paid to the organization or its creditors). Still, there is the potential for lost revenue during the transition to a new leader; there is the cost of the key man or key woman policy itself. In other words, your ability to put a price on the contingency plan is critical to its success.

PREPARATION OF THE CONTINGENCY PLANS NEEDED

In the next chapter, we'll go into greater detail on the steps to contingency planning and how to communicate those plans. You and your organization must be aware of the plans you need once you've established your list of "what ifs," so that you can bring in the right people to help you. Contingency plans can range from succession plans to fire-escape plans, from lawsuits to layoffs, from staff losses to media attention. The list is long, but you need not be daunted by all of this. Most of these plans can be mitigated step-by-step with the help of a consultant, especially if you don't feel that your team currently has the expertise to address certain plans by itself.

CONTINGENCY PLANNING FOR EXPANSION

Contingency planning takes into account potential future occurrences that could be catastrophic for an organization.

If your church received 1000 new members this weekend, how would that impact you?

If orders for your product doubled tomorrow, how would that impact you?

If you had budgeted a loss in revenue but your nonprofit was given more money than it could spend, how would that impact you?

Things we've been hoping and praying for could happen—but would we be ready for them? Contingency thinking can also address plans for growth and expansion. If God answered your prayers, would your systems be able to sustain the increase? I'm convinced that in many cases, sustainability—not ability—is the limiting factor for organizational growth. If you can't sustain it, it's not likely that what you're hoping for will come to pass. If you really expect it, get a plan, so you're ready to sustain it when it comes!

This year, when we could no longer meet on weekends or in homes, we desperately needed a contingency plan for small groups. We had to have a way to support relationship-building and ongoing connectivity for our partners. Our contingency plan was to have groups meet electronically. Our small groups are free society, so there is everything from golf to yoga to Bible study. In the recent pandemic, we couldn't do any of these wonderful things, but people still needed to connect. We recruited enough leaders so that everyone could connect with a few people weekly on a call and share personal stories, be encouraged, and pray together.

In closing, know this:

- The contingency plan won't be the same as the original plan.
- The contingency plan may not be as complex as the original plan.
- The contingency plan may not be as pretty or high-tech as the original plan.
- The contingency plan may produce greater results than the original plan.

We can make many plans, but the Lord's purpose will ultimately prevail. When we look back, we may just realize that the contingency plan was the Lord's plan all along!

CHAPTER 11

THE ELEMENTS OF A CONTINGENCY PLAN

Every leader must prepare for the days of uncertainty that lie ahead. While we feel this uncertainty most powerfully during crisis, the truth is that, even when we don't feel it, it's there. Scott Leshinski states, "Leaders in every industry are preparing to make critical business decisions during a time of uncertainty that is rapidly evolving before our eyes."

Contingency planning has been happening for thousands of years, and there is always going to be a need for it in the future. Let's take some time to examine the instances of contingency planning in the Bible.

HOW WAS CONTINGENCY PLANNING USED IN THE BIBLE?

In the unlikely event that God actually sent a flood, even though it had never rained, Noah built something that would be adequate for the situation: a boat that could hold hundreds of species of animals and enough food for two months. Whether you believe in this account or not, you have to admit that it's a powerful example of contingency thinking. Let's take a look at God's instructions to Noah in Genesis 6:14-17:

Make for yourself an ark of gopher wood; you shall make the ark with rooms, and shall cover it inside and out with pitch. This is how you shall make it: the length of the ark three hundred cubits, its breadth fifty cubits, and its height thirty cubits. You shall make a window for the ark, and finish it to a cubit from the top; and set the door of the ark in the side of it; you shall make it with lower, second, and third decks. Behold, I, even I am bringing the flood of water upon the earth, to destroy all flesh in which is the breath of life, from under heaven; everything that is on the earth shall perish (NASB).

Contingency thinking is demonstrated on Noah's part—and his plan saves lives. Here are three elements of contingency thinking that we can see in this story:

A flood was an unlikely event, yet there was sufficient reason to plan for it.

Noah had a detailed plan directly connected to the potential event.

The failure to have developed a detailed contingency plan would have been catastrophic.

This account is helpful because it mirrors many of the scenarios that leaders face today. There may be no evidence of a future risk other than a message received, a potential unseen threat, or an alert from another organization's experience. The flood, from a purely practical perspective, was an unlikely event, just like many of the events that require contingency thinking on our part. A detailed plan was put into place, with its only merit being in the event that the flood actually occurred. However, had Noah not acted on the message and built the ark, his family would have perished along with all the animals. Contingency thinking isn't new; it's been in play since the world began.

PRACTICAL APPLICATIONS OF CONTINGENCY THINKING

There's a good chance that you're already utilizing some level of contingency thinking. If you have insurance on your vehicle, your home, or yourself, this is an indication of this kind of strategizing. You are planning for a future event even though it hasn't happened yet. Let's walk through some other examples that you should be considering if you are not.

Bankim Chandra Pandey writes, "The leader should start with what can he do if the organization suffers a set back due to natural calamities such as flood, earthquake, accidental fire or if there is a loss of data due to cyber threats, loss of employees due to economic catastrophe and loss of brand image due to degradation in quality of product, inventory and supply chain problems."[16]

Ms. Pandey is proposing that leaders begin contingency planning by considering obvious potential risks instead of those that are low in probability. In this section, we will think through some of these potential risks. You'll see that you've already begun to employ contingency thinking by considering some basic negative risks. I am hopeful that this section will lead you to also apply these theories to positive possibilities and, ultimately, upgrade your plans.

Wills, Living Wills, and Estate Planning

You and each member of your team should already have a will and a living will in place. I know too many leaders who have created irreconcilable issues by dying or becoming ill and having no written direction for others. This is the lowest level of contingency thinking because death is not an unlikely event. Death happening within the next few hours is unlikely, but make no mistake—it will come. I pray that infirmity will never strike you or your team, but living wills should be in place now. It's likely that, if you're a senior-level leader, you've already addressed this, but your organization can be thrown into chaos if an important team member hasn't properly planned for the possibility of sickness, the certainty of death, and the hope of retirement.

As another part of your contingency process, your organization can add helps such as key leader insurance. This policy bridges the financial gap organizations often face with the premature loss of a high-level leader. Your financial advisor or organizational consultant can help with the details.

Some contingency thinking is complex and may require a great deal of expertise, but at the end of the day, you're looking at a visit to a lawyer or a few hours of work. Don't procrastinate!

Succession Planning

William Vanderbloemen said, "Every pastor is an interim pastor." Let's broaden that statement. Every leader is an interim leader! Next, he went on to say, "Thinking about what's next before they have to—that's what marks the greatest leaders, business people, athletes and politicians of the world.... Thinking about that transition ahead of time might make all the difference in your and your church's (organization's) legacy."[17]

It's never too early to begin the conversation and develop plans for what comes next. While this conversation must be held with a select few people, it does need to happen. Leaders who fail to plan for their futures, and the futures of their organizations, put everyone in a precarious position. If you wait until you see the need to plan, it's too late. Succession is another place to apply solid contingency thinking.

Emergency Communication and Evacuation Plans

Your organization should have a written plan for how communication takes place when there is a catastrophe, such as a natural disaster or a terrorist attack. Your team should know who to look to for direction and information. If there are public meetings, that information should be distributed to every leader in those gatherings. Additionally, there needs to be written evacuation plans that your guests services, security team, and others fully understand and for which they take ownership.

This is a higher level of contingency thinking than a living will or succession plan. This type of planning impacts more people and must have broader buy-in. Perform an audit this week of what you currently have in place, and determine next steps for bringing these plans up to standard.

NEXT STEPS

"Contingency plans can only be created for identified risks, not unidentified or unknown risks. Since, if you don't know what your risk is, it's impossible to plan for it. It should be noted that contingency plans are not only put in place to anticipate when things go wrong. They can also be created to take advantage of strategic opportunities. For example, you've identified that a new training software should be released soon. If it occurs during your project, you may have a contingency plan on how to incorporate it into the training phase of your project."[18]

Hopefully, you're seeing that our discussion of contingency thinking is designed to help you apply thoughtful strategy to the potential opportunities that come your way.

Life Science Leader founder David Walsh shares five concrete steps to developing appropriate contingency plans:[19]

- Program Management

- Planning
- Implementation
- Testing and Exercise
- Plan Improvement

While each organization has its own version of the planning process, most agree that some form of all the above are necessary. Use what you feel is applicable to your culture. Let's look at each one in turn.

Program Management

Every team must start somewhere. Many of us commence with a contingency team. This team may have representatives from several areas of influence within your organization; it should help senior leadership determine what areas will be reviewed. The beginning of the proposal-writing process should rest on this group.

Planning

The Planning Team, or its derivative, should work through the timeline for the implementation of any contingency plans. They then communicate that timeline to everyone involved. This team also keeps everyone accountable to time and date commitments for making progress on the plan(s).

Implementation

The contingency plan should spell out clearly who (both internally and externally) gets notified regarding those plans, and in what order they are to be notified. The people working on the ground are most affected by the event, so they need information that enables them to take immediate action. Each contingency plan should be implemented individually, not jointly, because of the level of detail and focus required for each.

Testing and Exercise

Take each plan through testing and exercise. Only then will you discover how well the plan works and its needs for improvement. For plans that cannot be tested without replicating a catastrophic event, you should walk through them in detail as if they were happening.

Plan Improvement

As your team performs tests and exercises, keep copious notes. Come back to planning meetings ready to develop strategies for improving each plan and all the associated systems.

USING CONTINGENCY TO LEVERAGE OPPORTUNITIES

When you're accustomed to contingency thinking, your organization is better prepared to leverage risks and take advantage of economic and cultural change. If you and your team can shift your focus from speculating on the negative to speculating on growth opportunities, phenomenal change can happen.

During our recent crisis, there were things we had wanted—but that crisis forced to happen. Crisis provides the opportunity for the growth of your vision and mission. In the Chinese language, the word for crisis is *weyjin*. It's actually comprised of two words: *danger* and *opportunity*. The Chinese language affirms that, in every crisis, there is both. Finding the danger is easy; finding the opportunity is difficult.

During crisis, our online presence was about 4,000 people every weekend—three times what it had been before. During crisis, we fed 1,500 people every weekend in two hours, as compared to 250 people in six hours before the crisis. Are you starting to see the lessons that crisis teaches us?

Look into the future and imagine what could go right; then, develop a plan that will be needed if things go that way.

CHAPTER 12

LEVERAGING THE LESSONS LEARNED

It's not the least coincidental: Adversity is a birthing place for greatness. People rise to their best when trouble comes, and as they rise, they begin to believe that anything is possible. The desperation produced by storms, disease, terrorism, war, and other tragedies produces leaders and leadership strategies. In times of peace, leadership and its principles are important, but in times of adversity, these principles are beyond important—they carry life-and-death potential. The power of context, collaboration, communication, and contingency are multiplied when used together.

Think about it: You become keenly aware of your context during crisis—where you are and with whom you're connecting. You work with partners to collaborate and multiply your reach. You communicate within your sphere, utilizing the strategies we've outlined. Because of contingency thinking, you even have a plan for future risks.

When you begin to think of these four principles together, there is a great deal of synergy. Each area requires you to think through your plans, look for strengths in others, share effectively in your sphere, and keep your heart and plans open for what may happen next. John Kotter discusses some aspects of this synergy and describes with some detail what he thinks the successful organization of the future will look like.

One particular characteristic he discusses is the "persistent sense of urgency." "Major change is never successful unless the complacency level is low. A high urgency rate helps enormously in completing all the stages of the transformation process." The four attributes of leadership we've discussed are designed to increase urgency and minimize complacency. The "kiss of death" in times of crisis is complacency. Urgency is the order of the day, every day. People are in need. Leadership is flexed. Resources are uncertain. And things don't change every day—they change every *hour*. Out of this chaotic blend of service and power, leadership is forged that, if properly utilized, produces real progress in the absence of crisis. Once again, it's true: Even when the crisis isn't global, *someone* is facing crisis. Those in your sphere need you to lead them as if you are in crisis, because so much of their well-being is dependent on it.

Let's take a final look at each of the 4 Cs, and review some major points about how they impact our leadership and organizations.

THE POWER OF CONTEXTUALIZATION

As we've discussed, context is the sum total of all that surrounds the sphere in which you're leading. It speaks to the demographics of communities, the economic and educational institutions, and the conditions in which people live. Contextualization, then, means understanding how people think, communicate, and make decisions. These facts don't change—no matter how much we pray or preach or push!

How well do you understand your context? Have you given any real time to thinking through exactly whom you're reaching and thus, whom you're called to reach? You are leading where you are because you've been uniquely equipped—designed, even—to thrive there. The better you understand your surroundings, the more effective you'll become. Your sense of context will improve the effectiveness of your communication, show you how to collaborate, and lead you toward contingency plans.

A deeper understanding of your context will also give you something that can't be measured in dollars and cents— something intangible but valuable: You will become more passionate about the people in your sphere, more concerned about their needs, and more ready to strategically plan for meeting those needs.

THE POWER OF COLLABORATION

In every context, there exists a certain level of trust or mistrust. More often than not, this trust level has direct ties to those who are presently involved in leading. You learn quickly during difficult times that little can be accomplished where there is a low trust level. "When trust is low, change is slow and costly, when trust is high then change is faster and less expensive."1 The word "change" can be used interchangeably here with the word "progress" or "success." When you properly contextualize the sphere in which you are called to lead, you must account for and assess the trust level. Once you make that assessment, you can build on the trust that exists and improve the trust wherever you discover a deficit.

The true sign of having addressed issues of trust is collaboration. Nothing helps us get past our mistrust and serve together like a major crisis. Suddenly, we see that our needs are greater than our own resources—our human resources, our financial resources, our intellectual resources, and so on. Crisis tends to amplify the reality that we all truly need one another in order to succeed. If your organization asks itself these three important questions, it can change your trajectory:

- What are we wanting to do that we don't have the resources for?
- What are we doing that we could do better if we collaborated?

- What have we stopped doing that we could have continued to do with help from a strategic partner?

Here's the lesson crisis has taught me about collaboration: *When what needs to happen is bigger than your ability, go get help!*

THE POWER OF COMMUNICATION

Normally, the discussion about communication begins with the message, but crisis has taught me that my message is not as important as understanding those *for whom* my message is intended. The message may change, but your target does not. Knowing your audience may actually adjust your message!

Communication isn't talking or writing—it's the exchange of information between two or more entities. Like its sister term, community, it can't exist or be measured in isolation. Communication must be examined by all parties, and measured based on how accurately information has passed from one to the other.

Begin with internal assessments: Does your organization know and understand the vision and mission? Do those who work, serve, or lead on the team recognize how they contribute to the mission? Can your entire leadership team communicate the vision? How far would you have to go in your organization before you found someone who *didn't* know and understand the vision? What you're attempting to determine is the depth of your communication culture.

When you look outside of your organization, you'll find the message spoken by your culture. Just as words frame culture, culture frames the words spoken about you. If you truly have a culture of kindness, outside people will make comments about how kind you are; if your culture is critical and judgmental, the words spoken in the community about you will indicate that. Remind your team members that they are your most watched "billboards!" If you communicate a servant's heart to your community and collaborative partners, it will open doors that narrow communications close.

THE POWER OF CONTINGENCY THINKING

The difference between good leadership and great leadership is the ability to be ready for what an uncertain future holds. Greatness is the result of building in enough robustness to handle the contingencies of life. In my leadership journey, the things I failed to plan for have impeded my progress the most. The old saying, "A failure to plan is a plan to fail," is accurate. Jesus even taught that when you get ready to build or go to war, there must be prior planning involved if you want to be successful. Contingency thinking plans for what could potentially happen.

No matter if the situations ahead are potentially bad or potentially good, we need a contingency plan that goes into effect when those events happen. America, like many other countries, had no definitive contingency plan for how it would respond if a pandemic-level virus were to hit its shores. The early church had no plan for what it would do if three thousand people were saved in one day. Whether it's a global pandemic or a local revival epidemic, your organization must be forward-looking and prepared.

Begin with contingency thinking in traditional areas, such as having adequate insurance, a will, a living will, succession plans, and emergency evacuation plans. If you start with these fundamental areas, they will equip you to formulate other, more complex plans down the road.

I'm a firm believer in this: No matter how much rain falls, the volume of your bucket doesn't change! If there are increased sales, donations, conversions, and opportunities coming your way, you must foresee them and plan for them. This is the rare but painful beauty of crisis. Dr. Lance Watson said it best in a talk I heard him give: "Fear always sees the danger in crisis. Faith always sees the opportunity in crisis." That is consistent with the Chinese word for crisis that is literally translated *opportunity* and *danger*.

Crisis, at its core, can be summarized by the words of Bobby Herrera in his book, *The Gift of Struggle*. Herrera uses the acronym VUCA, which stands for Volatility, Uncertainty, Complexity, and Ambivalence. Crisis produces all of these responses in exaggerated ways. Let's take a look.[20]

Volatile. Crisis can feel like a powder keg—a bomb that could go off at any time. It brings high highs and low lows. Crisis is enough to overwhelm the best of us.

Uncertain. Crisis leaves us unsure about what will last, when things will change, and whom we can trust. We're not clear on how long the crisis will last and if we'll outlast it. This can be unnerving to the core.

Complex. There seem to be few simple answers during calamity. The solutions being given by most people were acceptable during peacetime, but now most of them don't work. People look to leaders for answers to complex questions, while leaders themselves are scrambling to process and understand what's happening around them.

Ambivalent. Nothing is black and white during a crisis. The gray haze of ambivalence is the overarching color during these times.

"It was critical that we learn how to handle the stress we might encounter in combat situations...when there is a lot of chaos. We learned quickly that without the awareness of the stress that VUCA brings it could paralyze the team and the results would be fatal." VUCA helps a leader accept the occupational emotional hazards of the job and, by anticipating them, manage those emotions.

THE OTHER SIDE

On the other side of crisis, we find ourselves better prepared emotionally for the difficulties that follow it. Post-traumatic Stress Disorder, or PTSD, is the symptomatic response felt after we have lived through seasons of extreme stress. The body responds to stress in different ways for different people. Once crisis is over, some recover quickly, while others take a long time to heal. Leaders live with stress daily, and how we cope with that stress will impact the way in which we lead. If we can truly learn from the stress of crisis, we can put ourselves in a strong position.

This means we begin to see danger as a place of opportunity instead of solely a threat. A potentially volatile situation becomes an opportunity to bring peace. Uncertainty provides a chance to bring answers that can mitigate the unease. And, complex scenarios set us up to produce simple answers to myriad questions. Ambivalence puts the leader in a place to help his or her people.

Crisis has equipped us to lead like never before. It makes us into women and men who better understand our contexts and the people we are destined to influence. We learn to communicate clearly and concisely within our organizations and beyond them. This positions us to collaborate at higher levels and increase our influence through everyone we touch. We learn to think based on contingencies—what could potentially happen. We better prepare for the unknown because we now know how to develop plans for what could be. Your greatest opportunities are ahead of you! They may appear dangerous, but never forget: *Faith sees the opportunity in crisis!*

ENDNOTES

1. *The Speed of Trust: The One Thing That Changes Everything,* by Stephen M.R. Covey

2. Ibid.

3. *Five Levels of Leadership,* by John C. Maxwell

4. Quoted in *The Speed of Trust: The One Thing That Changes Everything,* by Stephen M.R. Covey

5. *Stress in Success,* by Sam Chand

6. *Dictionary.com*

7. *Hero Maker: Five Essential Practices for Leaders to Multiply Leaders,* by Dave Ferguson and Warren Bird

8. *The Me I Want to Be: Becoming God's Best Version of You,* by John Ortberg

9. *Dictionary.com*

10. *Passing the Leadership Baton: A Winning Transition Plan for Your Ministry,* by Tom Mullins

11. *Dictionary.com*

12. *Dictionary.com*

13. *New Thinking New Future,* by Sam Chand

14. *Dictionary.com*

15. *https://www.huronconsultinggroup.com/insights/contingency-planning-market-uncertainty-strategic-modeling*

16. *Contingency Planning—Transformational Leadership,* by Bankim Chandra Pandey

17. *Next: Pastoral Succession that Works,* by William Vanderbloemen and Warren Bird

18. *https://www.lifescienceleader.com/doc/the-steps-of-contingency-planning-0001*

19. Ibid.

20. *The Gift of Struggle: Life-Changing Lessons About Leading,* by Bobby Herrera